Let's Look Forwards

Let's Look Forwards

A Scriptural Guide
to the Major Landmarks
that precede Jesus' Second Coming

Simon Bennett

First edition 2017

P O Box 10375, Fourways, Johannesburg 2055, Gauteng
letslookforwards@gmail.com

The Author has made every effort to trace and acknowledge sources/resources/individuals. In the event that any images/information have been incorrectly attributed or credited, the Author will be pleased to rectify these omissions at the earliest opportunity.

ISBN 978-1-920-59258-5

For all who look for a brighter future,
And for Natasha
Thank you always for your love, encouragement,
and support on our journey
and for this project in particular.

Landmark

Noun

1. *An object or feature of a landscape or town that is easily recognized from a distance, especially one that enables someone to establish their location*

Synonyms: marker, mark, indicator, signal, beacon, lodestar, sign

2. *An event or discovery marking an important stage or turning point in something*

Synonyms: turning point, milestone, watershed, critical point, historic event

CONTENTS

We also have the prophetic message
as something completely reliable,
and you will do well to pay attention to it,
as to a light shining in a dark place,
until the day dawns and the morning star rises in your hearts.
2 Peter 1:19

Introduction

Have you been at a dinner or a meal with family or friends when an unwelcome topic comes up? Perhaps it concerns an event that's caused you or others great embarrassment. The room grows silent, people toy with the food on their plates, everybody feels uncomfortable and the pleasant atmosphere dissipates like air from a balloon. Finally, someone steers the conversation away from the taboo subject onto safer ground. You can sense the relief throughout the room. People start eating and drinking again, conversation picks up, and smiles return to faces. There is a general sense of "Whew! Thank God we're off that topic!" Everyone is relieved that they don't have to discuss *that*!

There is a similar reaction in mainstream Christian circles concerning the subject of Jesus' Second Coming and the events leading up to it. Consider conducting an experiment and bring it up. I think you might find some anxious looks, some shuffling of feet, and clearing of throats. The conversation will be short lived, with usually a solitary comment along the lines of, "No one knows the day or the hour."

It's a topic that makes people uncomfortable for two reasons: Firstly, members of our Christian family frequently embarrass us by announcing the return of Christ on a particular date. This is tremendously frustrating! We try to demonstrate the love of God, the truth of God and the sovereignty of God and His Word to the work; then someone embarrasses us by making a false statement that frankly makes us all look like idiots; it's so unhelpful!

At the same time, there are critical divides in the theological world, so we've no authoritative teaching to turn to. We can speak with great authority on Gospel matters. We can sound the trumpet loudly and clearly concerning salvation and the finished work of the cross. These topics all make for great sermons and exciting conversation.

However, when it comes to the return of Jesus, our theology is less clear. The trumpet sound trails off and there is uncertainty. After all, we don't know when He's coming back; 'it could be today, it could be tomorrow, it could be next year or it could be in a thousand years time!' Hence, it's not a 'safe' topic of conversation. We don't really know what to say about it, even when someone comes up with yet another outlandish prediction. It's a topic that we would rather steer clear of!

This, however, isn't true for me. As a young Philosophy, Politics and Economics student at Bristol University I became aware of two things. The first was my own brokenness and complete inability to fix myself. The second was, similarly, the brokenness of the world and its inability to fix itself. Both needed redemption and both needed a saviour. Both were in denial if they thought they could muddle through without one!

I was fortunate enough to meet Christians who could explain to me both God's plan for my redemption through the cross, and His plan for the redemption of the world through the Second Coming.

Both of these theologies amazed me. Firstly, that God should know my deep need and provide the exact remedy through His unconditional love on the cross, exchanging my sinful nature for his sinless one. Secondly, that He should see and recognise the brokenness of the world and show us and teach us the detail of how its redemption would occur. The teaching was complete. I was stunned that it all came out of this amazing old book – the Bible. I was ready to commit myself completely to a God who knew my present, past and future and that of the world. He held both in His hands and communicated fully about both in Scripture.

I would like to introduce the Second Coming as a topic of conversation once again. Perhaps you've also recognised not only your own brokenness but the brokenness of the world around you. And as a result you hunger afresh for the complete redemption of all things. I assure you that God won't disappoint you with His provision for you in Scripture.

In the following pages, I hope to whet your appetite once again for the prophetic in the Bible. I hope you'll learn, like me, to rejoice in a God who knows the future and loves to share vital snap shots of it with His children for their encouragement, edification and guidance.

Surely the Sovereign Lord does nothing without revealing
His plan to His servants the prophets.

Amos 3:7

Chapter 1

Are We Looking Forwards Clearly?

So, you must also be ready.....

Matthew 25:44

Are we looking back so much that we can't look forwards clearly?

Looking forward to what lies ahead....
Philippians 3:13 (TLB)

It's a classic home movie blooper clip. A man is taking a photograph on a pier by the sea. He is trying to get everyone into the frame. He takes several steps backwards as he adjusts the camera lens. Then he takes a final step, topples over the edge, and lands up in the water! He was so focussed on looking back at his subjects that he was unable to look in the direction he was going.

The Jews of Jesus's time suffered a similar fate. They loved the Law so much, and rightly so. As David said, *The Law of the Lord is perfect converting the soul* (Psalm 19). It was a wonderful, beautiful and life enhancing gift from God. But somehow as they focused on the Law, they lost sight of something better, the fulfilment of the Law, Jesus Christ. While focussing their eyes on what was in the past, they found they were unprepared for what was coming. They then literally 'fell over' the person, Jesus, who was the fulfilment and ultimate reflection of the Law.

He is the Stone that some will stumble over,
and the Rock that will make them fall.
1 Peter 2:8 (TLB)

Today we love the Gospel! It gives us life and light. We're reconciled to God and we've received a heavenly inheritance that we can enjoy today because of it. The Gospel is the most scandalously beautiful thing that God has gifted us through Jesus Christ. We love to feast our eyes, hearts and minds on it. We can't stop talking about it; and rightly so!

However, the church is largely silent on what is to come: the fulfilment of the Gospel, the Second Coming of Jesus and the events that will lead up to it. As the Law pointed the Jews towards the coming Messiah (Matthew 5:17), the Gospel points us towards the final physical manifestation and fulfilment of the kingdom of God.

However, in mainstream circles, it's rare to hear a sermon or Bible teaching on this topic. The church appears content to look backwards at the Gospel, but has little appetite to look forwards to its fulfilment.

In Jesus' time, there were Jews who looked forwards. While loving the Law and looking back at it, they were expectant and looked forward to the fulfilment of the Law. They studied the Scriptures about the coming of the Messiah and they were ready. Simeon and Anna in Luke 2:34-38 had their eyes focussed forwards expectantly. Unlike the Pharisees, they didn't stumble or fall over the Rock when He appeared. They were prepared and ready to acknowledge Him and proclaim the news of His arrival.

Coming up to them at that very moment, she (Anna) gave thanks to God
and spoke about the child
to all who were looking forward to the redemption of Israel.
Luke 2:38

What about us today? Are we so determinedly focussed on the Gospel that we're unprepared for events that will lead to the fulfilment of the Gospel? Are we knowledgeable about the God given Scriptures that will enable us to recognise and teach others about perhaps the greatest event in Biblical and world history? Or are we in danger of looking back so much that we have neglected to look forwards?

Flight Safety

We also have the prophetic message as something completely reliable, and you will do well to pay attention to it....

2 Peter 1:19

Before a passenger flight takes off, a standard procedure is followed. After everyone has found their seats, stowed their luggage in the overhead compartments and fastened their seatbelts, the crew takes up their positions for the safety demonstration. Instructions are given to passengers so that they will know what to do should the plane lose cabin pressure or make an emergency landing. Laminated cards with illustrations are provided. Even though no-one expects the plane to have problems, it is considered it a sensible and wise precaution to pay a modicum of attention to the safety procedures.

Perhaps this is an illustration of what our attitude should be towards the Scriptures concerning the Second Coming. Just as we aren't obsessive about safety instructions on the aeroplane, we don't need to be obsessive about Christ's return. Life goes on. However, it's another matter to ignore the safety instructions that He has provided for us in Scripture for those times.

In 2 Peter 1:19, Peter advises us that '*we will do well to pay attention*' to God's instructions concerning the Second Coming, so that in the event He does return in our lifetime, we can be secure in Him and ready.

Discernment

.... but can ye not discern the signs of the times?

Matthew 16:3 (KJV)

Soon after my wife and I were married, we opened our home in the UK to outgoing and returning missionaries. We offered them a base while they either finalised arrangements to go abroad or took stock upon returning from the mission field.

On one occasion a lady staying with us was emotionally vocal around the house. My reserved British nature found this difficult and was keen to take action. However, because managing conflict isn't my strong suit, I prayed to see how I should proceed. I was led to not proceed at all. The Lord impressed upon me that this lady was one of His best and bravest 'soldiers' who'd been 'wounded in battle'. I immediately felt a God given love and compassion for her. Instead of a desire to 'deal with her', I knew I needed to support her, as the Lord did.

Discernment from the Holy Spirit flipped my attitude. My eyes were opened to see things God's way, which was contrary to my own reasoning (Isaiah 55:7-8). As a result, I was able to respond helpfully and positively to the situation.

In Matthew 16:3, Jesus lamented the inability of the Pharisees and Sadducees to properly discern the signs of the times. Despite their training in the Scriptures, they doubted Jesus' authenticity. They questioned the One who was the very manifestation of the Word of God in their midst. They lacked discernment.

Anna and Simeon in Luke 2 were both filled with the Spirit of God. They were able to discern who Jesus was and responded appropriately. They didn't run around anxiously, trying to persuade everyone that the Messiah had arrived. They carried a spirit of faith and rejoicing.

Discernment is a gift of the Spirit that we'll need as we read Scriptures about the Last Days. These Scriptures can't be read with our own wisdom. We need to be filled with God's Spirit, to firstly believe the Word of God, and then to properly discern its application to the times we are living in.

Prayer: Lord Jesus. Fill me with Your spirit as I read, so that I may believe the Scriptures you have given in Your Word. Please, also give me the gift of discernment to properly discern how to apply these Scriptures to my life and to the world around me. Help me then to respond positively with faith and rejoicing. In Jesus' Name. Amen.

So, what exactly are we building on?

For no one can lay any foundation other than the one already laid, which is Jesus Christ.
1 Corinthians 3:11

When my wife and I were looking to buy our first house, we found one in Tempsford, Bedfordshire, UK. We swiftly made an offer that was accepted. However, before the sale went through, a surveyor was instructed to check the structure of the house. He spotted a tiny crack in a wall and diagnosed a serious problem of subsidence. The house was built on clay soil that swelled in wet weather and contracted when it dried. It would need expensive underpinning and we were advised that it wasn't a wise investment. The foundations weren't firm and would subside over time.

When considering the theology of Jesus' return, we are faced with a similar building problem. With Scriptures found throughout Ezekiel, Isaiah, Daniel, Nahum, the Gospels, the letters of Paul as well as Revelation, where do we begin building our theology? Where do we lay the initial boundary lines? Where do we dig the foundation so that we can be assured that our theology won't suffer subsidence with the passage of time?

John G Lake, a renowned American evangelist to South Africa in the early twentieth century, came up with what I believe is a sensible Scriptural solution. He stated that though all Scripture has authority, the words of Jesus have supreme authority. In US society, a decision in a District Court can be appealed to the Supreme Court.

The decision in the Supreme Court has decisive authority over all other courts. Likewise, when there is a lack of clarity in Scripture, we must appeal to the supreme authority of the words of Jesus. Though '*prophecies may fail*' (1 Corinthians 13:8), Jesus promised "*My words will never pass away.*" (Matthew 24:35)

We start with Jesus' words. His teachings lay the foundation and delineate the initial blue print for building. They will provide the support for the load-bearing walls of Second Coming prophetic Scripture. His words and instructions have to carry the weight of Scripture from the Old Testament, the Epistles and Revelation because only they can! (1 Corinthians 3:11)

In Matthew 24:3 Jesus' disciples asked, "*Tell us, when shall these things be and what shall be the sign of thy coming, and of the end of the world?*" Matthew chapters 24 and 25 provide an overview of last days' events with advice of how to prepare for them. It makes a good foundation for our study and our theology.

This teaching is known as the Olivet Discourse. There are similar accounts in the Gospels of Mark and Luke. We use Mathew for two reasons. First, it is an eye-witness account, as Matthew was present during this teaching. Second, it is the fullest version, encompassing 97 verses, compared to 37 in Mark and 31 in Luke. The full text of Matthew 24, describing the crucial landmarks, can be referred to in the appendix.

Summary of Chapter 1

Are We Looking Forwards Clearly?

1. We should look forwards to Jesus' Second Coming as well as looking backwards at the cross (Philippians 3:13).
2. We should pray for a Spirit-filled discernment *of* the Scriptures and a Spirit-filled response *to* the Scriptures (Matthew 16:3).
3. The supreme authority of the words of Jesus make them the best place to start building our theology (Matthew 24:35).

Chapter 2

The Landmarks of Matthew 24

So likewise ye, when ye shall see all these things,
know that it is near, even at the doors.
Matthew 24:33 (KJV)

On the Mount of Olives

And Jesus went out, and departed from the temple: and His disciples came to him for to shew him the buildings of the temple. And Jesus said unto them, See ye not all these things? Verily I say unto you, There shall not be left here one stone upon another, that shall not be thrown down.
And as He sat upon the Mount of Olives, the disciples came unto him privately, saying, Tell us, when shall these things be? ***And what shall be the sign of thy coming, and of the end of the world?***
Matthew 24:1-3 (KJV)

The disciples asked Jesus two questions in verse 3.

1. "When shall these things be?" This refers to Jesus' previous statement concerning the Temple buildings. "Verily I say unto you, there shall not be left one stone upon another that shall not be thrown down." Jesus was referring to the event in 70 AD when the Roman legions invaded Israel and destroyed the temple.

2. "What will be the sign of your coming and of the end of the age?" This question refers to Jesus' Second Coming.

There is perplexity as Christians try to determine which part of Jesus' answer refers to which question. Jesus Himself makes no distinction in His reply. There's mystery and tension here, but a solution will be revealed as we study the passage.

False Prophets

And Jesus answered and said unto them,
Take heed that no man deceive you.
For many shall come in my name, saying,
I am Christ, and shall deceive many.
Matthew 24:4-5 (KJV)

For many of us the first thing that comes to mind when we think of warnings of Jesus's return, is a man carrying a sandwich board with the words 'THE END IS NIGH!' emblazoned on it. As he stands alone, somewhat dishevelled, we feel rather sorry for him, until he levels his voice at us and the world in general with a message of judgement and anger. Or we think of religious groups who've ordered their members to sell their possessions and spend the night, dressed in white, encamped on the roof of their houses waiting for Christ to appear. They were certain that the time and date of Christ's return had been revealed to them, but were sadly mistaken.

Jesus repeats three times in Matthew 24 that false prophets and Christs, 'anointed ones', will arise and deceive many in the times before His return.

Many shall come in my Name, saying I am Christ and shall deceive many. (vs 5)

And many false prophets shall rise and shall deceive many. (vs 11)
For there shall arise false Christs, and false prophets,
and shall shew great signs and wonders;
insomuch that, if it were possible, they shall deceive the very elect. (vs 24)

I think we are familiar with one type of false prophet. He or she prophesies prematurely regarding the Second Coming. Paul recognized this type of false prophet and wrote a warning to the Thessalonians,

Don't let anyone deceive you in any way, ***for that day will not come until the rebellion occurs and the man of lawlessness is revealed.***
2 Thessalonians 2:2-3

Paul warned that Christians shouldn't be disturbed or deceived by false prophecies concerning Jesus' return. We should be able to measure them against God-given Scripture. In this passage, for instance, Paul refers to the revelation of a **'man of lawlessness'** as an important landmark that must occur before the Second coming.

Without a knowledge of Scripture, however, Christians can only shrug their shoulders and say to concerned friends, "We don't know! He could come any time!" We lack Scriptural knowledge to counteract false prophets that we see or hear of around us

There is another type of false prophet in Scripture, opposite in nature, though equally dangerous. In the times before the Babylonian invasion, Israel was plagued with false prophets, who prophesied continued peace, success and prosperity to Israel, even when dark days were approaching. They did it because the people told them to,

"Don't tell us the truth; tell us nice things; tell us lies. Forget all this gloom..."
Isaiah 30:10 (TLB)

The people didn't want to hear anything upsetting and the prophets obliged. They refused to preach words of warning from God. God called these prophets,

Dumb (mute) dogs who cannot bark.
Isaiah 56:10 (KJV)

Guard dogs bark to warn of impending danger. God's leaders are also to warn His children and the nations from His Word, not always proclaiming worldly prosperity and peace.

Paul also warns of this type of false prophet in another passage concerning the return of Christ:

When people are saying, "Everything is peaceful and secure," then disaster will fall on them as suddenly as a pregnant woman's labour pains begin.
1Thessalonians 5:3 (NLT)

Perhaps you can see both types of false prophets in today's' world: the wild and woolly individual who is always saying, "It's going to happen THIS year!", and the smooth-talking politician, pastor or motivational speaker whose only message is peace and prosperity.

The only antidote to the confusion that will be brought on by both types of false prophet is a thorough knowledge of the God-given Scriptures. His word will be the only reliable measure of truth and error that can sustain us through these times.

Birth Prep

For nation shall rise against nation, and kingdom against kingdom. There will be famines and pestilences and earthquakes in various places. ***All these are the beginning of birth pains.***

Matthew 24:7 (NIV)

My wife is a doula, or birthing partner. She loves to talk about the natural processes of labour. The contractions and the passage through the birth canal benefit the baby and prepare it for life outside the womb.

A wise mother prepares diligently for the time of labour. She studies carefully the various stages that her body will pass through. She gears herself up mentally and emotionally for the process that will culminate in her baby's birth. She recognises that fear is an enemy that will slow down her body's ability to cope with the contracting of the womb. On the other hand, trusting in the natural processes, that provide everything needed for the mother and baby, will hasten her labour. Like an athlete preparing for a race, she is excited because she can see the finish line and the precious treasure that will be hers when she crosses it.

Jesus likens the events leading up to His return, wars, earthquakes, famines and pestilences, to the beginning of birth pains. In other words, they will be the initial signs of a challenging time for the world and for the church.

We can prepare for Jesus' return with the same diligence and anticipation as a woman preparing for the birth of her baby. If we read and grow familiar with the Scriptural handbook that God has provided, we won't be surprised or overwhelmed by the 'labour process', as '*if some strange thing is happening to us*!' (1 Peter 4:12) Instead, we'll be able to endure difficult times, looking forward with joy and anticipation to the awesome conclusion, 'the birth', the return of our Lord and Saviour, Jesus Christ.

"Are we there yet? How much longer?"

They called out in a loud voice, "How long, Sovereign Lord, holy and true?"

Revelation 6:10

"How much longer?" "When will we be there?" Children plague their parents with such questions as they go on holidays or on visits to friends or family. The questions start when you've barely driven out of the driveway and they continue with increasing frequency as you near the long awaited destination. "Are we there yet?" "How much longer?"

I remember as a child taking the seemingly endless drive from London to our cottage in South Wales. As the journey became tedious, my older brother and I bickered and fought in the back seat. Our mother would promise us an apple when we reached the Membury Services, a rest-stop near Newbury, that was roughly the halfway point of the journey. Our eyes would scan the horizon as we searched hopefully for the tall radio mast that overlooked the Services.

A landmark that was closer to our destination was the two-and-a-half-mile journey across the Severn Bridge that marked the border into Wales. We knew we had to cross this engineering wonder before we could arrive at our destination. These landmarks helped us not be so agitated and provided some certainty during what seemed like an interminable journey. "Are we there yet?" How much longer will it take?"

Similar questions were also on the lips of the early disciples and continue to be in the hearts of all who seek the better country and happier citizenship that Jesus' Second Coming will bring. Jesus knew the curiosity of His disciples and anticipated the long wait that future Christians would endure as they looked forward to His Second Coming.

Like my mother, Jesus decided to help His children by providing landmarks that would help them recognise when their journey was drawing to an end. My mother never predicted the exact time of arrival and nor does Jesus (Matthew 24:36). But He does provide important landmarks. We can also scan the horizon for these events feeling secure and certain that what we've been told is sufficient for us on our journey.

What are the landmarks that Jesus predicted? In Matthew 24:4-13 He begins by relating some general landmarks such as wars, earthquakes, pestilences, false prophets and persecutions. However, Jesus soon becomes specific. He relates that He will come immediately after a time of unprecedented tribulation or trouble (Mathew 24:29-31), that will occur after the Gospel has been preached in the whole world as a witness to all nations (Matthew 24:14).

Here is the Matthew 24 text, with the landmark events highlighted and numbered:

*14. **And this gospel of the kingdom shall be preached in all the world for a witness unto all nations; and then shall the end come.** (1)*
*15. **When ye therefore shall see the abomination of desolation, spoken of by Daniel the prophet, stand in the holy place,** (whoso readeth, let him understand:) (2)*
16. Then let them which be in Judaea flee into the mountains:
17. Let them which is on the housetop not come down to take anything out of his house:
18. Neither let him which is in the field return back to take his clothes.
19. And woe unto them that are with child, and to them that give suck in those days!
20. But pray ye that your flight be not in the winter, neither on the Sabbath day:
*21. **For then shall be great tribulation, such as was not since the beginning of the world to this time, no, nor ever shall be.** (3)*
22. And except those days should be shortened, there should no flesh be saved; but for the elect's sake those days shall be shortened.
23. Then if any man shall say unto you, Lo, here is Christ, or there; believe it not.
24. For there shall arise false Christs, and false prophets,

and shall shew great signs and wonders; insomuch that,
if it were possible, the shall deceive the very elect.
25. Behold, I have told you before.
26. Wherefore if they shall say unto you, Behold, he is in the desert;
go not forth: behold, he is in the secret chambers; believe it not.
27. For as the lightning cometh out of the east, and shineth
even unto the west; so shall also the coming of the Son of man be.
28. For wheresoever the carcase is, there will the eagles be gathered together.
29. ***Immediately after the tribulation of those days***
shall the sun be darkened, and the moon shall not give her light, and the
stars shall fall from heaven, and the powers of the heavens shall be shaken:
30. ***And then shall appear the sign of the Son of man in heaven: and then***
shall all the tribes of the earth mourn, and they shall see the Son of man
coming in the clouds of heaven with power and great glory*. (4)*
31. And he shall send his angels with a great sound of a trumpet,
and they shall gather together his elect from the four winds,
from one end of heaven to the other.

Matthew 24: 14-31 (KJV)

Please, take the time to read through these Scriptures carefully. Examine them for yourself. Let them speak to you personally. Read the passages over several times. Imagine you're a traveller standing in awe in front of the Grand Canyon. You wouldn't rush past. The stunning view compels you to stop, examine and take stock of it. Similarly take the time to allow yourself to be imprinted by the power of Jesus' words in Matthew 24. This is His view of the future and should be ours too.

In simple terms, an itinerary based on the words of Jesus looks like this:

Landmarks to be passed before Christ returns

1. The Gospel preached in All the World (Matthew 24:14)
2. The Abomination of Desolation (Matthew 24:15-20)
3. The Time of Tribulation (Matthew 24:21-29)
4. The Second Coming of Christ (Matthew 24:30-31)

Take some time to let your eyes adjust to the landmarks of 'abomination of desolation' and 'tribulation' that Jesus predicts will precede His coming. Re-read the passage several times allowing God to speak to you through it. Pray for faith to believe that Jesus says it as it is, and as how it will be.

As our world heads into unprecedented times of change, I can happily stay busy, even if I don't know 'the day or the hour of Christ's return.' In the back–pocket of my mind, I keep this list of basic landmarks. They remind me that we're not quite there yet.

"You'd better be good! Jesus could come back tomorrow!"

That day will not come until... the man of lawlessness is revealed.

2 Thessalonians 2:3

Throughout the ages preachers have exhorted their congregations with the words, 'Jesus could come back tomorrow!' This contradicts not only the itinerary we have seen in Matthew 24, but also a specific instruction from Paul.

Paul gives a clear landmark in his second Epistle to the Thessalonians. He warns us that we won't arrive at our destination, that Jesus won't come back, until a certain *man of lawlessness* is revealed.

Don't let anyone deceive you in any way, ***for that day will not come***
until the rebellion occurs and the man of lawlessness is revealed,
the man doomed to destruction. He will oppose and will exalt himself
over everything that is called God or is worshiped,
so that he sets himself up in God's temple, proclaiming himself to be God.
Don't you remember that when I was with you I used to tell you these things?
And now you know what is holding him back,
so that he may be revealed at the proper time.
For the secret power of lawlessness is already at work;
but the one who now holds it back will continue to do so
till he is taken out of the way. ***And then the lawless one will be revealed,***
whom the Lord Jesus will overthrow with the breath of his mouth
and destroy by the splendour of his coming.
2 Thessalonians 2:3-8

Paul tells us this '*man of lawlessness*', also known as the Anti-Christ (1 John 2:18), will sit in the temple of God '*proclaiming himself that he is God*'. This Scripture also informs us that this ultimate bad guy will be defeated by Jesus at the very moment of His Second Coming.

And then the lawless one will be revealed,
whom the Lord Jesus will overthrow with the breath of his mouth
and destroy by the splendour of his coming. (vs 8)

Despite this Scripture, some academics insist that the Anti-Christ is an historical figure. Although, indeed there've been several prototype 'anti-Christs', (Nero, Hitler, Stalin) this Scripture clarifies that there will be a 'final-edition' Anti-Christ. His demise must coincide with Christ's return, qualifying him uniquely as the Anti-Christ of the end of days.

Again, examine the Scriptures for yourself. Read them several times. We can now share these Scriptures with those who say that Jesus can come back *any day*. No, Jesus can't and won't because the *man of lawlessness* must first be revealed.

We can add this landmark event from 2 Thessalonians 2 to our list.

Landmarks to be Passed Before Christ's Return

1. Gospel preached in All the World (Matthew 24:14)
2. The Anti-Christ Revealed (2 Thessalonians 2:3-8)
3. Abomination of Desolation (Matthew 24:15-20)
4. Time of Tribulation (Matthew 24:29)
5. The Second Coming of Christ (Matthew 24:30-31)

Shucks! Did I miss my turn?

Some remove the landmark...
Job 24:2 (KJV)

While driving, and especially when I'm in deep conversation, I can become oblivious to where I am on my journey. After a debate or discussion has subsided, I will, with a start, refocus on the highway or motorway and wonder where I am and whether I've missed my exit. A momentary panic grips me, as I realise that I have no idea where I am on the journey. I don't recall if I've passed the landmarks that will define when I'd arrive at my destination. Have I missed them completely? Where exactly am I?

I often wonder the same thing when listening to certain pastors and theologians discussing Jesus' return. Many argue that we've already passed the landmarks that we have just read about in Matthew 24. They say that the abomination of desolation and the tribulation have already taken place, and that the Anti-Christ has come and gone.

Theologians refer to an event in 70 AD when Roman legions under General Titus invaded Israel, destroyed the Temple and killed up to 1.2 million Jews. Do these events represent the abomination and tribulation that Jesus warned about? Is the Anti-Christ therefore an historical figure of a bygone era? Are there no landmarks left to prepare us for the climactic Biblical and Gospel event of the ages? Could Jesus therefore really come back any day?

Here are four Scriptural reasons why we still need to be looking out for these landmarks today:

1. In Jesus' narrative, the abomination of desolation comes *after* the Gospel has been preached in all the world as a witness to all nations.

> ***And this gospel of the kingdom shall be preached in all the world for a witness unto all nations; and then shall the end come.*** *When ye therefore shall see the abomination of desolation, spoken of by Daniel the prophet, stand in the holy place*
> **Matthew 24:14-15 (KJV)**

Seeing we recognise that the job of preaching the Gospel is ongoing, the abomination of desolation, according to the Scriptural narrative, is still to come.

2. Jesus said that this time of tribulation would be the most troublesome time the world will ever see.

> *For then shall be great tribulation,* ***such as was not since the beginning of the world to this time, no, nor ever shall be.*** *And except those days should be shortened, there should* ***no flesh be saved****: but for the elect's sake those days shall be shortened.*
> **Matthew 24:21-22 (KJV)**

This time period will threaten the very existence of mankind. It's so serious that if it weren't shortened '*no flesh would be saved*'. Can that verse describe the events in Israel in 70 AD?

Since then we've seen both the First and Second World Wars. In the latter over 60 million people were killed. Surely these were times of greater trouble than the Augustinian invasion of Israel.

The times Jesus talked about are on an almost unbelievable scale. With technological developments in the twentieth century, world-wide conflict could now lead to such a scenario. For these reasons, it seems unwise to conclude that the times of tribulation predicted by Jesus have already passed.

3. Jesus tells His disciples that He will return 'immediately' after the tribulation of those days. Other translations use the words 'soon after' or 'following'.

__Immediately after the tribulation of those days__ shall the sun be darkened, and the moon shall not give her light, and the stars shall fall from heaven, and the powers of the heavens shall be shaken: And then shall appear the sign of the Son of man in heaven: and then shall all the tribes of the earth mourn, __and they shall see the Son of man coming in the clouds of heaven__ with power and great glory.

Matthew 24:29-30 (KJV)

It's a stretch to say that close to 2,000 years could in anybody's mind constitute '*immediately*'. Are we able to take Jesus at His word? If so, He will return immediately after this time of intense tribulation. We must conclude that this time of tribulation is still to come.

4. The man of lawlessness described by Paul will be destroyed by Jesus when He returns.

And then the lawless one will be revealed, whom the Lord will consume with the breath of His mouth and destroy with the brightness of His coming.

2 Thessalonians 2:8

This Scripture tells us of a final clash between the lawless one, otherwise known as the Anti-Christ, and Jesus. It rules out the possibility that this *man of lawlessness*, could be an historical figure, because Jesus' Second Coming must coincide with his destruction.

A straightforward reading of these Scriptural narratives indicates that we've not yet passed the final landmarks of abomination and tribulation. They're still on the road ahead of us and need to be acknowledged and anticipated, if the church is to be prepared for these times.

I can see the mountains!

In your patience possess ye your souls.

Luke 21:19 (KJV)

As a child, driving towards the Alps was a memorable experience. Our family was in its way to a skiing holiday. When I first saw the mountain range in the distance, I was so excited! "We're going to be there soon!" I exclaimed, "After all, I can already see the mountains!" Three hours later we still had not arrived at our destination. It was so frustrating! The gorgeous snow covered peaks were so inviting and yet so elusive, no matter how many hours we drove! It just took so long to get there and I needed patience!

It's similar with Biblical prophecy. Throughout the ages Christians have seen 'the mountains', the signs that Jesus talked about in the early part of Matthew 24; famines, pestilences, earthquakes, iniquity abounding and love growing cold, false teachers and false prophets, persecutions, and tribulations. They assumed that Jesus was coming in short order! When they looked up years later, they found that Jesus still hadn't come back! So frustrating! This is why a more detailed understanding of the Scripture is helpful. With Scripture, we can counsel those who are impatient as to why they shouldn't presumptuously announce an impending Second Coming.

Another thing about mountains is that they can look remarkably similar and follow similar patterns. One can easily be mistaken for another as they rise and fall in similar fashion. You think you've arrived at one mountain, but actually the one you're really looking for is across another expansive and time-consuming valley floor. Once again this can be so frustrating for expectant travellers, weary after a long journey!

Human history can be the same. Patterns repeat themselves like rows of mountain peaks. Starting with Rome and the Caesars, many mountains have passed that perhaps initially might have appeared to fulfil the Scriptures. But Jesus hasn't yet come back, indicating that although the Scriptures may have been partially fulfilled, the final fulfilments or 'mountains' are still to come.

Perhaps this is why Jesus gave one answer to the disciples' dual questions at the beginning of Matthew 24. Because the patterns were similar, one answer suited both the 70 AD invasion and the Second

Coming. The first was a prototype of the second. However, the detail of the language in Matthew and Thessalonians prohibits us from concluding that we've already passed these landmarks. We must deduce that we are still to pass one final towering landmark mountain range before Christ's return.

But let's not be guilty of jumping to conclusions and making impetuous predictions. Like mountains in front of us, the fulfilments of these last days landmarks may not come as soon as we think or in the way that we think. Let's therefore stick to the word of God in our discussions and teachings.

How will God's Story End?

We must through much tribulation enter into the kingdom of God.
Acts 14:22 (KJV)

Like most people, I love a good story. It helps if the story has a good beginning, a good middle and a good ending. The ending is the most important! There's nothing so unsatisfying as a story that has an inconclusive and weak ending. It leaves a huge sense of anti-climax. Conversely, a good story builds tension and reaches a resounding conclusion.

Biblical stories follow a similar pattern. God delights in setting up scenes with almost unbearable tension that are then resolved victoriously. To list a few: Isaac bound on the altar of sacrifice, Moses trapped in front of the Red Sea, blind Samson at the temple, insignificant Gideon facing the Midianite hordes, teenage David pitted against battle-hardened Goliath, Shadrach, Meshach and Abednego in front of the fiery furnace, elderly Daniel surrounded by lions, Jesus suffering and seemingly vanquished on the cross, shining Stephen under a hail of stones, imprisoned Paul writing about freedom in Christ and exiled John alone on Patmos. All faced the tension of humiliating defeat, before the sun rose on glorious God-given victory.

How will the greatest story ever told end? Some believe the church, will be whisked away from any potential tension, danger or tribulation by the return of Jesus, *before* the time of tribulation, and arrive in heaven untested.

However, the Scriptures in Matthew 24 tell us that the Second Coming of Christ will be preceded by some of the greatest tension the world has ever known, characterised by the abomination of desolation and the great tribulation.

Thus the greatest story ever told, of God and His children on earth, will finish with an epic climax. God, the great Story Teller, has written a suitable final script for His church. He'll provide the circumstances in which her faith, knowledge of His Word and commitment to Christ, will be tested and gloriously manifested for all to see.

These are they ***which came out of great tribulation,***
and have washed their robes,
and made them white in the blood of the Lamb.
Revelation 7:14

A Case for Simplicity

The unfolding of your words give light; they give understanding to the simple.
Psalm 119:130

On 14th October 1066, the battle of Hastings was fought. Duke William of Normandy had landed with his army in the south of England. Harold Godwinson, the Saxon King, recently victorious over the Vikings at the battle of Stamford Bridge, marched the length of England to oppose the invasion.

On arrival Harold set up his positions on top of Senlac Hill. Waves of Norman soldiers attacked but failed to penetrate the Saxon lines. It looked like Harold had won the day. The Normans then cleverly pretended to leave the field. The Saxons left the security of the hilltop to charge what they thought were fleeing soldiers. The Normans turned around and decisively won the battle. Harold died after taking an arrow in the eye and on Christmas Day 1066, William was crowned King of England. The Saxons lost the battle when they left the security of the high ground and were defeated in the valley.

There are several assaults going on today against the authority of the Word of God. Some of the attacks come from the outside sources of atheism and humanism that deride faith in the word of a sovereign and omniscient God. Some also surprisingly come from Christian sources that tell us the common man should not and cannot take the Word of God at face value.

The impression is given that only the most learned individuals can understand the Word of God. They will invite you down into the valley for prolonged discussions as to why you cannot trust the narratives of Matthew 24 and the other prophetic books. They'll tell you it's all so mysterious that it can only be interpreted by scholars; it's too complex for the general reader. They will say it's a mistake to even think you could understand any of these things. By the time you have finished talking with them you may agree! You've come down to the valley and ended up in confusion. You should have stayed on the high ground of simple trust in the Word of God.

It's through faith in the Word of God that we understand the mysteries of both our world and the kingdom of God.

By faith we understand that the world was framed by the word of God.

Hebrews 11:3

Augustine taught that it is through simple faith that we gain understanding.

Seek not to understand that you might believe;
but believe that you might understand.

Saint Augustine

Jesus Himself praised His Father that the truths about His Kingdom were revealed not to the religiously clever and learned but to the simple.

At that time Jesus said, "I praise you, Father, Lord of heaven and earth,
because you have hidden these things from the wise and learned,

and revealed them to little children.
Yes, Father, for this is what you were pleased to do."
Matthew 11: 25-26

Here is the translation from the Message Bible.

Abruptly Jesus broke into prayer: "Thank you, Father, Lord of heaven and earth. You've concealed your ways from sophisticates and know-it-alls, but spelled them out clearly to ordinary people.
Yes, Father, that's the way you like to work."

This is God's way, the way He likes to work; that ordinary people have access to Him, His wisdom and His knowledge through faith in His Word. Yes, it requires study and good Bible teaching to find the common threads that God weaves through His Word, but the explicit narratives should never be undermined .

So, beware of teachers and 'learned' men who would persuade you to leave the high ground where you take God's prophetic Word at face value. You may end up like the Saxons at the battle of Hastings, confused and defeated down in the valley. Instead, stay on the high ground, trust in the landmarks we've been given, and contend for the faith from there.

Lest your minds should be corrupted from the simplicity that is in Christ.
2 Corinthians 11:3 (KJV)

Pause

Before we move on to look at the detail of the final landmarks, we will:

1) Address our fears about tough times in Chapter 3 'Troubled?'
2) Read the good news of the return of Christ and the following events in Chapter 5 'The Return of the King.'
3) And look how the Olivet Discourse tells us to '*be ready*' in Chapter 6 'Preparations.'

Only then we will move on to study the landmarks of 'the abomination of desolation, 'the time of tribulation', and 'the Anti-Christ'.

Summary of Chapter 2

The Landmarks of Matthew Chapter 24

1. God's Word will provide us with a refuge of faith and certainty in tumultuous times when false prophets will abound. (Matthew 24: 5,11,24)
2. God's Word indicates a testing time before Jesus' return. Being prepared, like a woman preparing for giving birth, will greatly improve the church's ability to respond. (Matthew 24:7)

3. Jesus can't come back 'any time'. Jesus, in Matthew 24, and Paul, in 2 Thessalonians 2, give us landmarks that must be passed before Jesus returns:
    1) Gospel Preached in All the World (Matthew 24:14)
    2) The Anti-Christ Revealed (2Thessalonians 2: 6-8)
    3) Abomination of Desolation (Matthew 24:15-20)
    4) Time of Tribulation (Matthew 24: 21-29)
    5) Second Coming of Christ (Matthew 24:30-31)

    We now have a foundation for our end time theology. We can call into question interpretations and doctrines that do not align with the parameters laid out in Matthew 24.
4. Let's be cautions and wise about how we handle the Scriptures knowing that, like the mountains in the distance on a long drive, appearances can be deceptive. Let's therefore avoid unwise predications and conjectures. Let's rather stick to Scripture in our teachings and discussions. (Luke 21:19)
5. The narrative of Matthew 24 tells us God's story will end with a memorable and tension filled finale. (Matthew 24:15-29)
6. Staying simple, trusting His word, avoids confusion. (2 Corinthians 11:3)

Chapter 3

Troubled?

See that ye be not troubled

Matthew 24:6

Offence: The Dangers of Being Troubled

And then shall many be offended, and shall betray one another, and shall hate one another.

Matthew 24:10

Have you experienced offence? I know, on my part, all rational logical thought goes out the window when I am offended. I focus on troubling circumstances that I don't understand. My expectations have been dashed and I feel it's unfair! Suddenly all my Christian virtues evaporate and are replaced by bitterness and resentment. "It's just not right!" I think to myself as I try to justify my rising blood pressure. I inhabit a precarious place when I am so troubled that I give place to offence.

On Jesus' first visit to earth, many people were troubled and offended when He didn't live or speak according to their expectations. They were expecting an all-conquering king who would deliver Israel from the yoke of Roman rule. When Jesus disappointed them, offence took root, finally blossoming into the hate and betrayal that finally led to the cross.

Jesus warns us in Matthew 24 that many will be so troubled that they will '*be offended and shall betray one another and shall hate one another*'. The people of God will turn on each other! Once again, God will work out His plan and purposes contrary to man's natural expectations. Unprepared sections of the church are expecting to avoid the time of tribulation. They will be offended and troubled as the landmarks Jesus talked about come to pass. This will cause great division in the body of Christ.

Jesus tells us to '*see to it*' that we are *not* troubled or offended. We are to take care not to fall into that trap. If we know God's word, we can avoid these unrealistic expectations and that most precarious of places, the place of offence. We will be prepared.

Don't be Troubled

Jesus does not want us to be afraid or anxious. He recognises that the possibility of living during difficult times is daunting for all of us. How will we manage? How will we respond? Will we have enough faith? Will we be strong enough? As we examine our own ability and 'faith level', we often feel inadequate to face *any* difficult time and that troubles us! Does it have to be that way? Is there encouragement to be found in God's Word?

The following principles have encouraged me when I have felt troubled in these studies.

God will meet me at the level of my faith

Truly I tell you, ***if you have faith as small as a mustard seed,***
you can say to this mountain, 'Move from here to there,'
and it will move. ***Nothing will be impossible for you.***
Matthew 17:20

Probably my first reaction to difficult times is, "I don't think I have the faith for this." I look inward to my own faith, and doubt that it's sufficient. I start to fear and fret looking at some other outward help aside from what I feel is my small faith.

However, in Matthew 17:20, Jesus tells me I can move a mountain with faith as small as a mustard seed. His Word encourages me *not* to look at my own faith, but to keep my heart and eyes on the One in whom my faith lies. My faith isn't about what *I* can do, but what I can *trust* God to do.

My faith isn't the problem. The problem is that I am so ready to give away my faith and grasp onto my unbelief. Like the man who said, *I believe, I just have a problem with my unbelief!* (Mark 9:24), I have the tendency to believe my doubts and doubt my beliefs.

I should trust that the faith God has given me is sufficient. I must believe that the faith that helped me find a parking place this morning, is the same faith that will guide me in the days to come. The faith that brought me into my present position of employment is the same faith that will take care of me and supply my needs in the future. I don't need greater faith. I just need to apply the measure of faith God has given me to a bigger problem and not cast it away. God will meet me at the level of my faith.

So do not throw away your confidence (faith); it will be richly rewarded.

Hebrews 10:35-36

God will meet me at the level of my ability

My power is made perfect in weakness.
2 Corinthians 12:9

Looking through the Bible at men and women of God who went through times of trouble, I discover that God met them at the level of their ability.

After fleeing from Egypt, Moses was a shepherd in the Midian desert for 40 years. He learnt all about the patience required to lead a flock of sheep in the wilderness. It was just about all he did know. When the Exodus kicked off and the journey through the wilderness began, it was familiar territory for Moses. It was a time he had already been well prepared for over the preceding forty years. He was ready and equipped with wilderness experience. God met him at the level of his ability.

What did David do when he faced Goliath in the valley of Elah? He slung a stone. You might say, "*I couldn't do that!*" But David had been doing little else for years. He had spent his days watching his father's sheep, protecting them from wild animals. He had practised and practised with his sling-shot hundreds of times a day, for days on end. By the time God's opportunity arrived, he didn't need to do anything else other than what he had already been doing. God met him right there at the level of his ability.

What did Daniel do when he heard Darius's decree? He prayed as he had prayed all his life. From his youth, he had exercised his faith and spiritual disciplines no matter what circumstances he was in. When he heard the fateful decree from King Darius that would result in a trip to the lion's den, he opened his window and prayed the same as he had always done. Daniel stayed faithful to what he had always been doing. He prayed and God met him right there at the level of his ability.

None of these Biblical heroes did a double somersault or a triple salko. None of them were asked to do anything particularly new or foreign to them. God absolutely met them at their own level of ability and that is where He will meet me and you.

God will come through as I rest in the level of my own ability. Rather than being afraid of and covering up my weakness and inability, I need to be honest about these short-comings with Him and others. This will enable Christ's strength in me to come through. God will meet me at the level of my ability.

Therefore I will boast all the more gladly about my weaknesses, so that Christ's power may rest upon me... For when I am weak, then I am strong.

2 Corinthians 12:9-10

It's Your Job Lord, Not Mine!

The Lord will perfect that which concerns me.

Psalm 138:8 (KJV)

The ultimate encouragement is to know that it isn't my responsibility to see myself through difficult times. It is God's. I belong to Him.

He is the *author and the finisher of our faith (*Hebrews 12:2) and *will complete the work He has begun in me* (Philippians 1:6). I am *not my own, but have been bought with a price* (1Corinthians 6:20)

My job description is to trust Him, listen to Him and receive His guidance. Everything else is God's department and His concern, not mine! Moses was a junior partner in the business of the Exodus. All the hard work and heavy lifting was done by God. Similarly, I will be a junior partner in God's plan for me in a time of trouble.

Recognising this spiritual truth is vital. We've understood that we can't contribute to the work of redemption that Jesus did on the cross for our salvation. We must also recognise that apart from trusting, listening to Him and obeying Him, we cannot contribute to His work of keeping us through times of trouble! It will be His responsibility and His job, not ours! Keeping our eyes and minds on this principle will bring us peace.

You will keep him in perfect peace,
Whose mind is stayed on You, Because he trusts in You
Isaiah 26:3 9 (NKJV)

Trust in the Lord with all your heart; and lean not to your own
understanding. In all your ways acknowledge Him
and He shall direct your paths.
Proverbs 3:5-6 (NKJV)

Summary of Chapter 3

Troubled?

1. Jesus warns that many will be troubled and offended. (Matthew 24:10)
2. Jesus warns us not to be troubled by last days' events (Matthew 24:6)
3. God will meet us at the level of our faith (Matthew 17:20)
4. God will meet us at the level of our ability (2 Corinthians 12:9)
5. It's His job to bring us through, not ours. The Lord will perfect that which concerns us. (Psalm 138:8)

Chapter 4

The Return of The King

And they shall see the Son of man coming in the clouds of heaven with power and great glory.
Matthew 24: 30 (KJV)

The Turnaround

For He has rescued us from the dominion of darkness and brought us into the kingdom of the Son He loves.

Colossians 1:13

July 1985 was a difficult month for me. I'd returned to London after two years at Bristol University. In the economics exam in May, I'd found myself staring at a piece of paper filled with unintelligible questions. *Come on,* I said to myself, *you can write SOMETHING!* I reread the questions and had to admit I didn't understand any of them. Well, I wasn't going to sit around for three hours, so I got up, gave my empty answer paper to the invigilator and walked out into the sunshine.

What next? I felt I could never study economics again, not while there was this huge emptiness inside me. I'd spent much of the year questioning and was exhausted from thought, from endless rationalising. What was the purpose of life? What am I here for? Who am I? And what is going on with the rest of the world, rushing full of confidence, yet seemingly ignorant of where it was going?

I managed to get a temporary job in Victoria Street, Central London, working in the City Hall building. I don't recall the work, only the painful memory of utter hopelessness. Somehow, I was a fish out of water in this world, gasping for the air of some certainty, some direction and some affirmation. *Enough, enough!* I finally prayed, *God if you are there, help me find a way. Help me, please, because I can no longer help myself; I'm in despair.*

The next day I went to work as usual, lifeless. I wandered back from my lunch break, zombie-like. Suddenly my attention was drawn to a grinning man on a bench who was waving a large piece of paper in my direction.

Forty five minutes later, everything had changed... permanently. Nothing would be the same again. Christ and His Word had come in. Darkness gave way to light and death to life. My life was turned around as I received Christ and began to learn the truth about His plan for me and the world I lived in.

The world will experience this on a grand scale when Christ returns. The final days of tribulation will see great darkness.

Immediately after the tribulation of those days shall ***the sun be darkened****, and* ***the moon shall not give her light****, and* ***the stars shall fall from heaven****, and the powers of the heavens shall be shaken:*

Matthew 24;29 (KJV)

The sun will literally be darkened, the moon won't give her light and the powers of the heaven will be shaken. It will seem, I'm sure, like the end of the world – hopeless. However, the darkness will be shattered by a blinding light.

For as the lightning cometh out of the east, and shineth even unto the west; so shall also the coming of the Son of man be

Matthew 24: 27 (KJV)

In a moment the landscape will be transformed as Jesus appears in the clouds of Heaven, signalling glorious deliverance and final eternal reconciliation for His children. Believers will rejoice and celebrate. At last! Patience, faith and endurance will be rewarded by the sight of our Saviour returning. The turnaround will have finally taken place. But the people of the world, not recognising Jesus as Saviour, will mourn.

And then shall appear the sign of the Son of man in heaven: and then shall all the tribes of the earth mourn, and they shall see the Son of man coming in the clouds of heaven with power and great glory.

Matthew 24:30 (KJV)

He will send His angels to gather His children to Him.

And he shall send his angels with a great sound of a trumpet, and ***they shall gather together his elect*** *from the four winds, from one end of heaven to the other.*

Matthew 24:31 (KJV)

This once-in-the-earth's lifetime event is known as the Rapture. Jesus warns us to come to faith together, so people are not left behind.

Then shall two be in the field, ***the one shall be taken and the other left****. Two women shall be grinding at the mill;* ***the one shall be taken and the other left****. Watch therefore: for ye know not what hour your Lord doth come.*

Matthew 24: 40-43 (KJV)

Paul describes this event in 1 Thessalonians 4.

For the Lord himself will come down from heaven, with a loud command,
with the voice of the archangel and with the trumpet call of God,
and ***the dead in Christ will rise first.***
After that, ***we who are still alive and are left will be caught up***
together with them in the clouds to meet the Lord in the air.
And so we will be with the Lord forever.
Therefore encourage one another with these words.
1 Thessalonians 4: 16-18

All the saved will be resurrected; those who have already died will rise first and then those of us who are still alive. This will be the pay-off for the years of difficulty; to see Jesus face-to-face and be united with Him.

We can read about our reception in Heaven in full in Revelation 7.

Then one of the elders answered, saying to me,
"Who are these arrayed in white robes, and where did they come?"
And I said to him, "Sir, you know." So he said to me,
"These are the ones who come out of the great tribulation,
and washed their robes and made them white in the blood of the Lamb.
Therefore they are before the throne of God,
and serve Him day and night in His temple.
And He who sits on the throne will dwell among them.
They shall neither hunger anymore nor thirst anymore;
the sun shall not strike them, nor any heat;

for the Lamb who is in the midst of the throne
will shepherd them and lead them
to living fountains of waters.
And God will wipe away every tear from their eyes.
Revelation 7: 14-17 (NKJV)

Praise God! Reading these scriptures demonstrate to us that it will be worth it all when we see Jesus! The difficulties of the tribulation period will be swallowed up by the love, grace and glory of God.

It will be worth it all When we see Jesus, Life's trials will seem so small
When we see Christ. One glimpse of His dear face
All sorrows will erase So bravely run the race Till we see Christ.
Esther Kerr Rusthoi

The Party

Then the angel said to me, "Write this:
Blessed are those who are invited to the wedding supper of the Lamb!"
Revelation 19:9

There are the three distinct periods of a traditional Jewish marriage. The Hebrew terms for these periods are the Shiddukhin, the Eyrusin and the Nissuin*.

The Shiddukhin refers to the preliminary arrangements prior to the legal betrothal.

The Eyrusin refers to the period after the betrothal ceremony. The bridegroom leaves to prepare a place for his bride while the bride focuses on her personal preparations.

The Nissuin is the final step in the Jewish wedding tradition. Now the groom, with much noise, fanfare and romance, arrives at the bride's home to bring her to her new residence. The pinnacle of this joyful celebration is the wedding supper, set up at the house they will share. This is much more than just a sit down dinner for all the guests. It includes seven full days of food, music, dance and celebration. Now finally the couple will consummate their marriage and live together as husband and wife, fully partaking of all the duties and privileges of the covenant of marriage. *

Jesus's return to gather His church at the end of the time of tribulation will be followed by a 'wedding supper' in the Father's house.

For the wedding of the Lamb has come,
and his bride has made herself ready.
Fine linen, bright and clean, was given her to wear."
Then the angel said to me, "Write this:
Blessed are those who are invited
to the wedding supper of the Lamb!"
Revelation 19:7-9

If this is consistent with Hebrew tradition, it will be a celebratory party. Having appeared with great fanfare in the sky to collect us, He will whisk us away from the earth to our eternal home for the wedding supper. He will show us the '*mansions*', or living quarters, He has prepared for us, and will celebrate the glorious moment of our eternal union with a tremendous party. (John 14:2 KJV)

Keeping our minds and hearts on this heart-warming event will be so important as we face the times of difficulty that will precede His coming. We'll persevere through the time of tribulation knowing the wedding supper of the Lamb awaits us. He has been watching over us all the time, His heart pained by the difficulties we've faced. What joy there'll be for those of us, who've run and finished the race as we are united to Him!

*https://yeshuaarmy.wordpress.com/2012/06/04/the-marriage-feast-of-the-lamb-bjoern-jewish-wedding-customs-a-nd-yeshuas-return/

Awards Ceremony

Be faithful unto death and I will give you a crown of life.
Revelation 2:10b (NKJV)

Awards ceremonies are a huge deal in the world; the Oscars, the Grammy's, the Great British Bake Off, the X Factor; let alone all the sporting competitions, the Olympics, World Cups, etc. These competitions and award ceremonies seem to be essential to twenty-first century culture.

Scripture indicates that the greatest awards ceremony of all time will occur after the return of Christ as He publicly rewards His bride with special crowns and commendations.

Paul talks of Christians appearing before the Judgement Seat of Christ.

For we must all appear before the judgement seat of Christ;
that every one may receive the things done in his body,
according to that he hath done, whether it be good or bad.
2 Corinthians 5:10

The word used for the judgement seat is the Greek word, *bema*, a term given to the podium where the athletes would receive their rewards. Our sins, already paid for at the cross, are not an issue here. What will be judged is our works and service to Him.

Jesus is a generous judge. He promises that if we even give a simple cup of water to one of his little ones, we won't lose our reward (Matthew 10:42). Every act of love and sacrifice will have been recorded and will be rewarded. How blessed we'll be at that time!

Paul, however, advises us:

But each one should build with care. For no one can lay any foundation
other than the one already laid, which is Jesus Christ.
If anyone builds on this foundation using gold, silver, costly stones,
wood, hay or straw, their work will be shown for what it is,
because the Day will bring it to light. It will be revealed with fire,
and the fire will test the quality of each person's work.
If what has been built survives, the builder will receive a reward.
1 Corinthians 3:10-14

Will our works stand the test of time and have eternal value? To ensure they do, it's worthwhile to reflect on whether we are making the most of the Gospel opportunities available to us. In the light of the judgement seat, we should evaluate the Gospel impact of our daily lives on others. The Awards ceremony in Heaven will reveal it all.

Invasion – The End Game

Independence Day 1 is a movie about an alien force that invades earth. There's no doubt whose side you are on as the aliens raze multiple capital cities around the world. Brave humans rally their forces and penetrate the alien spaceship headquarters with a stolen alien fighter, disabling their defensive shield. A lone pilot then sacrifices himself to destroy the energy core of the spaceship and sabotages the whole invasion.

Exciting, rousing stuff! Revelation 19, however, speaks of an invasion that will end somewhat differently. After the celebrations at the wedding supper and the Judgement Seat, Jesus will gather heavenly forces to invade earth.

I saw heaven standing open and there before me was a
white horse, whose rider is called Faithful and True....
The armies of heaven were following him,
riding on white horses....
Then I saw the beast and the kings of the earth

and their armies gathered together to wage war
against the rider on the horse and his army
But the beast was captured...
Revelation 19:11, 14, 19, 20

After the Lord's victory in this final battle (found in full in Revelation 19 in the appendix), Satan is bound..

And I saw an angel coming down out of heaven, having the key to the Abyss
and holding in his hand a great chain.
He seized the dragon, that ancient serpent, who is the devil, or Satan,
and bound him for a thousand years
Revelation 20: 1,2

Meanwhile the saints will inherit the kingdom and rule and reign with Christ.

They came to life and reigned with Christ a thousand years
Revelation 20:4

This is the grand finale of all grand finales; the invasion and revelation of Jesus as King, Conqueror and Ruler, and the promotion of His children to reign with Him. It marks the beginning of a new era, the thousand-year reign of Christ on earth, often termed The Millennium.

Reading these Scriptures on The Return of Christ, the Wedding Supper and the Judgement Seat of Christ helps us rejoice in and to mediate on our relationship with Christ and our service to Him and others. These things also form the basis of Jesus' advice on how to prepare for these times

Summary of Chapter 4

The Return of The King

1. Jesus returns immediately after the time of tribulation (Matthew 24:30-31)
2. The saved church, both dead and alive, will be gathered up by angels and meet Jesus in the air (1 Thessalonians 4:16-18)
3. The saved church will then attend the wedding supper of the Lamb (Revelation 19:5)
4. And be rewarded at the judgement seat of Christ (2 Corinthians 5:10)
5. Jesus will then lead a heavenly invasion (Revelation 19: 11-20)
6. And start His thousand-year rule with the saints (Revelation 20:6)

Chapter 5

Preparations

The horse is prepared for the day of battle, but deliverance is of the Lord.

Proverbs 21:31 (NKJV)

Where am I? What am I doing?

The master of that servant will come on a day when he does not expect him.

Matthew 24:50

Since I left university after only two years of my degree, I've had a recurring dream. In it I find myself on a busy university campus. Everybody is one their way to lectures. I think, *I must find my lecture hall. Where is it?* I realise that I don't know where I am going, so I stop to ask a passer-by. He asks helpfully, "*What are you studying?*" I rack my brains and say helplessly, "*It's the funniest thing, but I can't even remember what I am studying!*". It dawns on me that I will face an exam soon and that I will fail as I can't find the lecture hall for a subject that I can't remember! When I wake up I am so relieved to find that it's one of those 'university' dreams again! It's unpleasant to face a testing exam when you are completely unprepared. It is stressful enough when you are prepared!

Scripture describes a very testing time before the Coming of Christ. Are we skilling up to prepare for such a time? Or are many unprepared for a time that Jesus has told us will be the most testing since the beginning of the world?

There's still time to prepare and to teach the necessary Word of God that will equip the saints for this final 'exam', a final testing experience. The passage of Scripture we've been studying is certainly challenging, however, at the end of Matthew 24, Jesus asks the question:

Who then is a faithful and wise servant, whom his Lord hath made ruler over His household, ***to give them meat in due season?***
Matthew 24:45

Faithful and wise servants will prepare and equip themselves and their households for these times: teaching them the solid, meaty, scriptures about the 2nd Coming. Only His word brings revelation, wisdom and strength. Only His word can shed light on the path ahead. Reading and internalising His word is therefore our first preparation for the testing times that are ahead.

Jesus' Advice in Matthew 24

What other preparatory advice does Jesus offer us in Matthew 24 (KJV): Let us look through the text and glean the instructive verses:

Verse 4: Take heed that no man deceive you...

How can we avoid being deceived? Knowledge of the Word of God, the only standard of truth, is our sole protection. God has given His church what she needs in Scripture.

Verse 6: See that ye be not troubled....

Know Jesus and His Word, so you aren't troubled.

Verses 15-20: These verses refer to the time of tribulation which will be addressed in greater detail in Chapter 7 'The Tribulation'.

Verse 26: Wherefore if they shall say unto you, Behold, he is in the desert; go not forth: behold, he is in the secret chambers; believe it not.

Know that Jesus will appear in the sky and not in the world.

Verse 33: So likewise ye, when ye shall see all these things, know that it is near, even at the doors.

Know the landmarks that Jesus described in Matthew 24.

Verse 42: Watch therefore: for ye know not what hour your Lord doth come.
Verse 44: Therefore be ye also ready: for in such an hour as ye think not the Son of man cometh.

Keep your eyes open: don't sleep; be ready.

Verse 45: Who then is a faithful and wise servant, whom his lord hath made ruler over his household, to give them meat in due season?

Share His Word. Preach and teach the Scripture.

Jesus' Advice in Matthew 25

Matthew 25 is the continuation of the Olivet discourse. In it, Jesus shares parables about His return.

The Parable of the Ten Virgins Matthew 25:1-13

Give us some of your oil. Our lamps are going out.
Matthew 25:8

In this parable five wise virgins have lamps that are full of oil. When the bridegroom arrives at midnight, they are ready to greet Him. The foolish virgins have no oil in their lamps and are turned away at the door by the groom with the words, "*I never knew you.*" They thought the bridegroom would come in the daytime and were unprepared for the hours of darkness.

We are to be prepared for dark times, our lamps full of oil, which represents the Spirit of God. When these times come, Spirit-filled people will be led by the Spirit and will find their way. Those unprepared with empty lamps, will be lost in the dark.

Firstly, we should first discern the times we live in. Scripture describes how 'darkness' will fall over the last days' landscape. Some of these scriptures, Matthew 24: 4-13; 2 Timothy3: 1-4; 2 Thessalonians 2:3; Daniel 12:4 and 2 Peter 3: 3-6 can be found in full in the appendix. We should pray for discernment from God's Spirit as we read them.

Many Christians, the five foolish virgins, do not discern the signs of the times. They do not recognize the falling darkness and therefore do not prepare.

Secondly, we must ensure then that our lamps are full of oil; that through word and prayer we have a close relationship with the Spirit of God that will sustain us through dark times. If we truly hunger and thirst for the Spirit of God, recognising that we are entirely insufficient in ourselves, and sincerely ask the Lord to fill us, He will. We should stay in fellowship with a good Spirit-filled church and learn how to be led by the Spirit in our daily life and interactions. The best way to ensure you will make important Spirit-led decisions in the future is to learn how to make Spirit-led decisions now. You can practice now, when the pressure isn't on. By the time darkness falls, Jesus teaches, it will be too late.

The Parable of the Talents or Bags of Gold: Matthew 25: 14-30

So I was afraid and went out and hid your gold in the ground.
See, here is what belongs to you.
Matthew 25: 25

Jesus tells the parable of the talents near the end of his Olivet discourse about His return. It tells the story of two successful investors and one failure. Two were active in trading their money and were rewarded. One buried his money in a hole in the ground and was fiercely rebuked and cast out. He tried to protect himself from his master's anger and ended up provoking it.

The primary work that Jesus has for His servants isn't in investing in the money markets, but in the Gospel realm. His servants are to be living, walking, talking examples of His Gospel and support in whatever ways possible Gospel work in their communities and the world at large.

In this respect our greatest safety will be investing our time, finances and lives in Gospel living and work. This is the way we will be in harmony with our Lord and 'save' our lives. This will help ensure a good outcome, not only when we meet the Lord at the judgement seat, but also in how we are led, protected and provided for in the difficult times leading up to His return.

Isaiah 58 beautifully describes the guidance and blessing that results when we help others less fortunate than ourselves.

> *If you extend your soul to the hungry, and satisfy the afflicted soul, Then you light shall dawn in the darkness, and your darkness shall be as the noonday. The Lord will guide you continually and satisfy your soul in drought, and strengthen your bones; You shall be like a watered garden, and like a spring of water, whose waters do not fail.*
>
> **Isaiah 58: 10-11 (NKJV)**

As Christians, we should continue living Gospel-centred lives, following Jesus and blessing our communities. There are wonderful promises in the Word of God for people who continue to 'lose' their lives for His sake through helping others. In losing our lives, Scripture says, we shall save them (Luke 9:24).

In the Parables of the Ten Virgins and the Talents, part of the Olivet discourse, Jesus emphasises spiritual rather than physical preparation. As we focus on His Word and the Holy Spirit, seeking first His kingdom, all other things will be added to us. If there are physical things to be adjusted, the Spirit will lead us to adjust them, in His way and in His time. The benefit of this approach is that it's always an effective and Godly way to live our lives, a win-win method for living, whether Jesus comes back in our lifetime or not. Hallelujah!

Summary of Chapter 5

Preparations

1. Be ready for these times (Matthew 24:44)
2. Know and share the Word of God (Matthew 24: 4, 45)
3: Be filled with the Spirit, surrendered to the Spirit, and learn how to be led by the Spirit (Matthew 25: 1-13)
4. Stay busy in Gospel living and work (Matthew 25:14-30)

Chapter 6

The Abomination of Desolation

When ye therefore shall see the abomination of desolation,
spoken of by Daniel the prophet, stand in the holy place,
(whoso readeth, let him understand).
Matthew 24:15 (KJV)

The Abomination of Desolation

All Scripture is God-breathed and useful for teaching... so that the man of God may be thoroughly equipped for every good work.

2 Timothy 3:17

Jesus predicted in Matthew 24:15 that the '*abomination of desolation, spoken of by Daniel the prophet*' would initiate a time of trouble before His Second Coming.

What do the words 'abomination of desolation' mean? What constitutes an abomination? The best English translation of the original Hebrew words is 'the desolating sacrilege'. Desolating means to cause complete emptiness or destruction. A sacrilege is the violation of a sacred person, place or thing, i.e. taking the Lord's name in vain is sacrilegious.

So, the abomination of desolation is something or someone that is sacrilegious and causes complete destruction. It is necessary to dig deeper on this, so that we can teach others about this crucial final landmark event.

Gabriel Pronounces a Heavenly Decree

While I was still in prayer, Gabriel the man I had seen in the earlier vision, came to me in swift flight about the time of the evening sacrifice.

Daniel 9: 21-22

The Angel Gabriel is a well-known Biblical character. As children, we learnt that he was sent to Mary to announce God's plan for the birth of the Messiah. (Luke 1: 26-38) We may know that he was also sent to Zechariah to tell him the good news that his elderly and barren wife Elizabeth was also to give birth to a boy (Luke 1: 11-26). Gabriel is known as God's messenger, entrusted with vitally important messages for mankind.

Surprisingly though, few are aware of Gabriel's two previous assignments, even though Jesus refers to one of them in Matthew 24. Gabriel appears to Daniel in Daniel 8:16 to interpret a vision. However, it is in Daniel 9:21 that he is sent to pronounce an historic prophetic decree that includes the 'abomination of desolation.' It is to this passage that we turn next.

Daniel had been praying for Israel and Jerusalem from Daniel 9 verses 4-19. Then Gabriel appeared and announced:

Daniel, I have now come to give you insight and understanding.
As soon as you began to pray, an answer was given,
which I have come to tell you, for you are highly esteemed.
Therefore consider the message and understand the vision.
Seventy 'sevens' are decreed for your people and your holy city...
Daniel 9:22-24

Gabriel's announcement is a decree. A decree is an authoritative order having the force of law. Gabriel is making a decree that carries the weight of heavenly authority and knowledge. Once it has been spoken, it will come to pass.

This is one of the most remarkable prophecies in scripture. It includes information about the crucifixion of Christ and the subsequent destruction of The Temple in Jerusalem by the Romans. It then concludes with detail about the abomination of desolation, predicted by Jesus to occur shortly before His Second Coming.

In full Gabriel's decree reads:

Seventy 'sevens' (seven year periods) are decreed
for your people and your holy city to finish transgression,
to put an end to sin, to atone for wickedness,
to bring in everlasting righteousness,
to seal up vision and prophecy and to anoint the Most Holy Place.
Know and understand this: From the time the word goes out
to restore and rebuild Jerusalem
until the Anointed One, the ruler, comes,
there will be seven 'sevens', and sixty-two 'sevens'.
It will be rebuilt with streets and a trench, but in times of trouble.
After the sixty-two 'sevens', ***the Anointed One***
will be put to death *and will have nothing.*
The people of the ruler who will come will destroy the city
and the sanctuary*. The end will come like a flood:*
War will continue until the end, and desolations have been decreed.
He will confirm a covenant with many for one 'seven'.
In the middle of the 'seven' he will put an end to sacrifice and offering.
And at the temple he will set up an abomination that causes desolation,
until the end that is decreed is poured out on him.
Daniel 9:24-27

The decree consists of seventy 'sevens' or seventy periods of seven years. The first sixty-nine 'sevens' deal with the coming of and crucifixion of the Messiah. You can discover the amazing fulfilment of this section of the decree in the appendix. However, it's the final seven-year period that we will turn to, because it contains information about 'the abomination of desolation'.

The Final Seven Years

He will confirm a covenant with many for one 'seven'.
In the middle of the 'seven' he will put an end to sacrifice and offering.
And at the temple he will set up an abomination that causes desolation,
until the end that is decreed is poured out on him.
Daniel 9:27

Gabriel decrees one final 'seven' or seven-year period relating to Israel. It's during this time that the abomination of desolation will be set up.

Using Daniel 9.27 as a base, we will now look at these questions concerning the abomination of desolation;

Who sets up the abomination of desolation?

When is it set up?

Where is it set up?

And finally, what is it?

Who Sets Up the Abomination of Desolation?
The Ruler who will come

He will set up an abomination that causes desolation...

Daniel 9:27

The twentieth century has seen several notably destructive leaders, who rose to power in their respective countries in times of great economic and social uncertainty. Although initially admired and acclaimed, Adolf Hitler, Josef Stalin and Chairman Mao were eventually all responsible for untold destruction and suffering.

The Bible speaks of one last leader, a man, who will take centre stage in the days before Jesus comes back. Here in Daniel 9:27 we read of him as the ruler who sets up the abomination of desolation.

The 'he' in Daniel 9:27 is '*the ruler who will come*' from Daniel 9:26.

The people of the ruler who will come will destroy the city and the sanctuary

Daniel 9:26

In 70 AD, after a Jewish rebellion, the Roman legions destroyed the city of Jerusalem and the Temple. The Romans are therefore ***the people of the ruler who will come***. This final last days' ruler will therefore in some way be related to the Romans or Europe.

His end is decreed as well:

*....**until the end that is decreed is poured out on him.***

Will his demise take place at the end of these last seven years? It appears so. We shall look at these timings in greater detail later. For now, it is sufficient to know that this final despotic ruler, who sets up the abomination of desolation, is somehow related to Rome or Europe.

When is the Abomination of Desolation? The Covenant

He (the ruler who will come) will ***confirm a covenant...***
Daniel 9:27

On September 30, 1938, Neville Chamberlain, Prime Minister of Great Britain, landed in England from Munich, Germany, in triumph. He carried with him a peace treaty that he had signed that day with Adolf Hitler.

The streets were so packed with cheering people that it took Chamberlain an hour-and-a-half to drive the nine miles to the Palace. After reporting to King George VI, Chamberlain and his wife appeared on the palace balcony. He then went to Downing Street, heading upstairs to address the crowd from a first-floor window. He announced, "I believe it is peace for our time."

Sadly this hope was short-lived. September 1, 1939, less than a year later, marked the start of World War 2 in which approximately 50 million people lost their lives.

Daniel 9 tells us of a similar agreement or covenant, that is confirmed for a period of seven years.

He will confirm ***a covenant*** *with many for one 'seven'.*

Daniel 9:27

In the middle of this seven year period, three and a half years after the covenant is confirmed, the ruler '*sets up the abomination of desolation*.'

In the middle of the 'seven' he *will put an end to sacrifice and offering.*
And at the temple he **will set up an abomination that causes desolation.**

Daniel 9:27

What is this covenant that the ruler confirms with many? The Hebrew word for covenant is *b'rit* meaning covenant, pact or treaty. This covenant is confirmed *with many.* This is an agreement between many parties.

In Daniel 11 the covenant is referred to three times, twice as the *Holy Covenant.* This indicates that the covenant may have some sort of religious connotation.

The king of the North will return to his own country with great wealth,
but his heart will be set against ***the Holy Covenant.***
He will take action against it and then return to his own country.

Daniel 11:28

He will return and show favour to those who forsake ***the Holy Covenant.***

Daniel 11:30

With flattery he will corrupt those who have violated ***the covenant.***
Daniel 11:32

Like the Munich treaty, this covenant is fragile. As we see in the three verses above, this leader's heart is set against it and he works with those who forsake and violate it. Finally, 'i*n the midst*' of the seven year covenant period, three-and-a-half years in, the ruler sets up the abomination of desolation is set up. This gives us the answer to the question 'when'? The abomination of desolation in the middle of a seven year period following the confirmation of a covenant or treaty.

We can also now add a new landmark to our list.

1. Gospel Preached in all the World (Matthew 24:14)
2. The Confirming of a Covenant for 7 years (Daniel 9:27)
3. The Anti-Christ Revealed (2 Thessalonians 2:3-8)
4. Abomination of Desolation Set Up (Matthew 24:15-20; Daniel 9:27;11:31)
5. The Time of Tribulation (Matthew 24: 15-20)
6. The Second Coming of Jesus (Matthew 24:29-30; Daniel 7:13; 2 Thessalonians 2:8)

The 2030 Agenda for Sustainable Development makes for important reading for those interested in the covenant of Daniel Chapter 9. Signed in September 2015 at the United Nations by 193 governments, it's, at the least, a prototype of what the Covenant may look like. You can read a summary of this Agenda in the appendix.

Where is the Abomination of Desolation?
The Jewish Temple Rebuilt

And ***at the temple*** *he will set up an abomination that causes desolation....*
Daniel 9:27

There are few places in the world quite like Jerusalem, the site of holy places for all three major religions, Judaism, Christianity and Islam. It's a focal point of the world's attention nearly 2,000 years after the crucifixion of Christ in 30 AD and the destruction of the Jewish Temple in 70 AD. At present it hosts the Dome of the Rock, Islam's holiest mosque and one of the longest running international disputes concerning the rights of the Palestinians to have partial sovereignty over this ancient city.

In Matthew 24, Jesus states that the abomination of desolation will stand in the Holy Place. This is a term used to describe the Temple in Jerusalem.

So when you see standing ***in the holy place*** *the abomination that causes desolation ....*
Matthew 24:15 (KJV)

In the book of Daniel, scripture is also specific about the location of the abomination; *at the temple* in Daniel 9:27 and *at the temple fortress* In Daniel 11:31.

And at the temple he will set up an abomination that causes desolation....
Daniel 9:27

His armed forces will rise up to desecrate the temple fortress
and will abolish the daily sacrifice.
Then they will set up the abomination that causes desolation.
Daniel 11:31

These Scriptures describe that Jerusalem and the Jewish temple will once more become a Biblical focal point, as the location for the setting up of the abomination of desolation. For these verses to be fulfilled, the Third Temple will need to be built and the daily sacrifice of the Temple instituted.

The following article from www. breakingisraelnews.com indicates that this is a realistic scenario.

We're Ready to Rebuild the Temple By Thuli Weisz 4/08/2014
Despite the tragic war Israel is currently entangled in, our generation has been blessed with the fulfilment of numerous Biblical promises. We have seen the rebirth of the State of Israel and continue to witness the Ingathering of the Exiles from the four corners of the world. For the first time in centuries Jerusalem is in Jewish hands, yet once a year, on the 9th day of the Hebrew month of Av, Jews fast, cry and mourn for the destruction of the Holy Temple. How can we ignore all these great blessings and why do we mourn for a building that was destroyed 2,000 years ago?

The Bible repeatedly describes the Temple as the spiritual centre of the world and the source for peace and prosperity. In Isaiah's famous vision the prophet describes, "They shall beat their swords into ploughshares... for my house shall be called a house of prayer for all nations. " The absence of the Temple is seen in the stories reported on the nightly news and its void adversely affects nations, geo-politics and global peace. Director of the Temple Institute in Jerusalem, Rabbi Chaim Richman explains that the 9th of Av 'is not about bemoaning the Temple. It's about bemoaning the world without the Temple. A world that has lost its light, its colour and its direction.'

Indeed, there is a growing 'Temple Movement' in Israel today with thousands of Jews working to rebuild the Temple. According to a poll taken last year in a leading newspaper Ha'aretz, one third of Israelis believe that Israel should erect the Temple on the Temple Mount. Israel's Housing Minister called publicly for the rebuilding of the Temple. "We've built many little, little temples." MK Uri Ariel said, referring to synagogues, "but we need to build a real Temple on the Temple Mount."

Schools throughout Israel are diligently studying the intricate laws of the Temple and Jews of all backgrounds visit the Temple Mount each month. The Jerusalem Post quoted Sarit Berko, a non-observant Israeli who came to the Western Wall to observe the 9th of Av from her home in Tel Aviv, an annual pilgrimage she has made since the six Day War in 1967. "During Passover, most Jews say 'Next year in Jerusalem'," explained Berko, "As an Israeli I pray, 'Next year may the Third Temple be built and last for eternity.'"

The Temple is such a central theme in the Bible that one third of all its commandments deal with laws carried out in it. Rabbi Richman explains that far from being an extremist, "our desire to see a rebuilt

Temple is an expression of healthy, normative Judaism."

While it is true that our generation has much to be grateful for and that our return to Israel is nothing short of miraculous, the golden dome sitting atop the Temple Mount provides a constant reminder that the Torah cannot be fulfilled perfectly and Judaism cannot be expressed fully until the Third Temple is rebuilt in Jerusalem.

It will take a remarkable resolution of the political and religious tension in the Middle East in order for the third temple to be built. Is it possible that the Holy Covenant will facilitate this?

In whatever way the rebuilding of the Temple takes place, we are able to add it as another landmark to our list and conclude that this is where the abomination of desolation will be set up.

Landmarks to be passed before Christ's Return:

1. Gospel Preached in all the World (Matthew 24:14)
2. Rebuilding of the Jewish Temple (Matthew 24:15; Daniel 9:27; 11:31)
3. The Confirming of a Holy Covenant for 7 years (Daniel 9:27)
4. The Anti-Christ Revealed (2 Thessalonians 2:3-8)
5. Abomination of Desolation Set Up (Matthew 24:15-20)
6. The Time of Tribulation (Matthew 24:21-28; Daniel 12:1)
7. The Second Coming of Jesus (Matthew 24:29-30; Daniel 7:13; 2 Thessalonians 2:8)

What is the Abomination of Desolation? 'You're gonna have to serve somebody!'

He sets himself up in God's temple, proclaiming himself to be God.
2 Thessalonians 2:4

Bob Dylan wrote and recorded *Serve Somebody* on his 1979 album *Slow Train Coming.* He sings in the chorus, 'It may be the devil, it may be the Lord, but you're gonna have to serve somebody.' He's saying that we can't inhabit a place where we serve nobody. Ultimately, all our lives consist of worship of some sort or another. Though many people believe themselves to be in a place where they worship nobody, Bob Dylan says no such place exists. 'It may be the devil, it may be the Lord, but you're gonna have to serve somebody!'

Throughout Scripture we find instances where populations are brought to points of decision about who they will serve. Elijah proclaimed to the gathered host of Israel on Mount Carmel, *How long will you waver between two opinions? If the Lord is God, follow Him: but if Baal is God, follow him* (1Kings 18:21). It was time to make a choice. There was no longer a middle ground option.

In Daniel 3 Nebuchadnezzar set up a golden image and demanded that it be worshipped. His herald announced that whoever did not bow down and worship the image would immediately be thrown into a blazing furnace. A choice had to be made! Shadrach Meshach and Abednego bravely refused to worship the image and were delivered from the furnace by the power of God.

The Scriptures we are about to read indicate that the abomination of desolation will precipitate a similar time of decision.

So what is this abomination of desolation? We find the term first in Daniel chapters 9 and 11.

And at the temple he will ***set up*** *an abomination that causes desolation*

Daniel 9:27

Then they will ***set up*** *the abomination that causes desolation.*

Daniel 11:31

The abomination of desolation is something that is set up.

Although we have found information about *who* sets it up, *where* it is set up and *when* it is set up, there is no further information in the Book of Daniel about *what* it is. We therefore turn to the Book of Revelation to see if there is anything that:

1. Is set up just prior to Jesus' return.
2. Is a desolating abomination or sacrilege.
3. Leads to a great time of trouble.

We read in Revelation 13:

It ordered them ***to set up an image*** *in honour of the beast.... It was given power to give breath to the* ***image of the beast****, so that* ***it could speak and cause all those who refused to worship the image to be killed.***

Revelation 13:14-15

An image will be *set up* – an image of *the beast*. (This beast is defeated by the returning Christ in Revelation 19: 19-20). This image that is set up will *speak*.

A talking image would've been a strange and unreal concept at the time when the Revelation was delivered in the first century, but with television and the internet, talking images that impact the world are now commonplace. This image will cause *all who refuse to worship it to be killed*. Reminiscent of Nebuchadnezzar's idol, this is the very definition of an abomination that will lead to an unprecedented time of great trouble.

The nature and timing of this image of Revelation 13 make it a prime candidate to be the abomination of desolation of Daniel 9 and Matthew 24. It's a sacrilege that occurs shortly before Christ's return, that leads to a time of great trouble.

Pauls' description of the final world leader in 2 Thessalonians reinforces this.

> *He will oppose and will exalt himself over everything that is called God or is worshipped, so that* ***he sets himself up in God's temple, proclaiming himself to be God.***
>
> **2 Thessalonians 2:3-4**

Therefore the Scriptures indicate that the abomination of desolation may well be an image of a world leader, set up in God's Temple prior to a time of tribulation. Like Nebuchadnezzar's statue in Daniel 3, death will be the consequence of refusing to worship it.

At that moment Bob Dylan's lyrics will quite literally be fulfilled:

'It maybe the devil, it may be the Lord, but
you're gonna have to serve somebody.' It will be time to choose.

Summary of Chapter 6

The Abomination of Desolation

1) The term abomination of desolation is found in Daniel 9:27.

2) It is part of Gabriel's seventy 'sevens' decree that also includes the crucifixion of Christ and the destruction of the Jewish Temple in 70AD.

Q: Who sets up the abomination of desolation?

A: A 'ruler' related in some way to Rome or Europe. (Daniel 9:26,27)

Q: When is the abomination of desolation set up?

A: In the middle of a final seven year period after the confirming of a covenant or treaty (Daniel 9:27).

Q: Where is the abomination of desolation set up?

A: Scripture points to it being in the Holy Place, the rebuilt Jerusalem Temple. (Matthew 24:15; Daniel 9:27, 11:31; 2 Thessalonians 2:3-4)

Q: What is the abomination of desolation?

A: It is something that is 'set up'; most likely to be the 'talking image' of a satanic world leader described in Revelations 13:14-15 and 2 Thessalonians 2:3-4.

CHAPTER 7

The Anti-Christ

Dear children, this is the last hour

and as you have heard that the antichrist is coming,

1 John 2:18

Rinse after taking.

And I went unto the angel, and said unto him, "Give me the little book. And he said unto me, Take it, and eat it up; and it shall make thy belly bitter."

Revelation 10:9 (KJV)

Growing up in the 1970's, being sick wasn't fun. As well as the discomfort and nausea of sickness, there was the medicine. Cough syrup was a dark foul tasting liquid that in no way rewarded me for being home in bed. It was a bitter medicine that motivated me to get better as soon as possible! The medicine was swallowed quickly, my mouth rinsed immediately and I hoped to be better before the next dose was administered!

As we study these final landmarks before Jesus comes back, it's rather like taking that medicine. Don't be surprised if you feel a little sick yourself. Bad news such as the abomination of desolation has that effect when we hear of it for the first time. It certainly made Daniel feel sick. After a dream of the future in Daniel 7, he admits that *his face turned pale.* After an end time vision in Daniel 8, he tells us he *lay exhausted for several days.* This is heavy material.

We do need to know about these events, but they aren't among the *pure, lovely, admirable and praiseworthy* things that Paul admonishes us to *dwell on* in Philippians 4:8. Jesus and His Word should fill our minds, not dark thoughts of future difficulties. Some people develop an unhealthy interest in the Last Days, that isn't balanced with the peace, faith and restfulness that result from a healthy walk with Jesus and His Word.

Just as I rinsed my mouth from bitter medicine, my mind also needs to be continually 'rinsed' with a healthy view of Christ, His grace, His promises and His continued sovereignty over our lives. It's crucial that we practice and maintain the habit of looking up to Christ and remind ourselves of His eternal promises and presence with us.

*And when these things begin to come to pass, **then look up**, and **lift up your heads**; for your redemption draws near.*
Luke 21:28 (KJV)

Anti-Christ: Fact or fiction?

The term Anti-Christ is well-known due to popular movies such as *The Omen* trilogy and *The Devil's Advocate.* In *The Omen,* the boy Damian, aided by a sinister nanny, cuts a swathe of supernatural destruction on his way to world domination. In *The Devil's Advocate,* Al Pacino, a top Manhattan lawyer, schemes to manipulate Keanus Reeves' character to father a child who will become the Anti-Christ.

Such tales make one wonder whether this character is actually a product of superstitious fiction rather than Scripture. Surely, he isn't actually a real person?

The Anti-Christ is in fact the central figure in Last Day's Scripture, appearing in the books of Daniel, Thessalonians and Revelation. In all three books, his demise coincides with the Second Coming, (2 Thessalonians 2:8; Revelation 19:19-20 and Daniel 7:11,13). He is an essential part of any study of Christ's return.

In Daniel 9:26,27 we have read of him, as '*the ruler who will come*', who will '*set up the abomination of desolation*'.

In 2 Thessalonians 2 we now read how he sets *himself up in God's temple claiming to be God.*

The Anti-Christ: A Masquerade

And no wonder, for Satan himself masquerades as an angel of light.

2 Corinthians 11:14

The child-catcher from *Chitty Chitty Bang Bang* is often voted best villain in children's movies in film polls. He didn't appear in the original book by Ian Fleming, but was the creation of scriptwriter Roald Dahl.

In the film the children of Vulgaria are held prisoner in Baron Bombast's castle. A child-catcher is sent out to search for two children who have just landed in the magical car. He returns from his first efforts empty-handed and so decides on a new approach. He disguises himself as a sweet merchant giving away free ice creams, lollipops, and treacle tart. The children fall for this deception, come out from the safety of their hiding place, and are captured.

Evil, masquerading as good, is uniquely disturbing. It is horrifying to watch as unsuspecting victims walk into a trap, deceived by a delusion of safety and security.

The Bible describes how a satanic world leader will arise and deceive the whole world into worshipping him.

This is Paul's description of him in 2 Thessalonians 2:

Concerning the coming of our Lord Jesus Christ...
Don't let anyone deceive you in any way,
***for that day will not come until the rebellion occurs** (1)*
***and the man of lawlessness is revealed** (2),*
the man doomed to destruction.
He will oppose and will exalt himself over everything that is called God
or is worshiped, so that he sets himself up in God's temple,
***proclaiming himself to be God** (3) And then the lawless one will be*
*revealed, **whom the Lord will consume with the breath of His mouth and***
***destroy with the brightness of His coming** (4).*
*The coming of the lawless one **is according to the working of Satan**(5),*
***with all power, signs, and lying wonders** (6),*
and with all unrighteous deception among those who perish, because
***they did not receive the love of the truth, that they might be saved** (7).*
2 Thessalonians 2:1, 3-4, 8-10

Here are the points that we can draw from the text:

1. He will rise in a time of rebellion from God.
2. Jesus will not come back until this man is revealed.
3. He will oppose God and sit in the Temple of God, claiming to

be God himself.

4. He will be defeated and destroyed by the Second Coming of Jesus.
5. He will act according to the working of Satan, and use all the ways that wickedness uses to deceive.
6. He will display power through signs and wonders.
7. The unsaved will be deceived because they have rejected the truth.

This passage in Thessalonians gives us several valuable pieces of information.

Most importantly, as we have already noted, this Scripture places him definitively at Christ's return. It isn't possible for Jesus to return *any day.* Paul emphasizes that Christ cannot return until this ruler *is revealed.*

Paul warns us that he will perform signs and wonders and act *accordance with the way Satan works.*

In the Garden of Eden Satan promised Adam and Eve freedom and education, but delivered bondage and death. In the wilderness he appeared to be concerned for Jesus' physical needs and offered Him *all the kingdoms of the world.* He cunningly turns unsuspecting humanity against a loving God until it is left with only one option – worship of Satan.

Like Satan and the child-catcher, the Anti-Christ will 'dress up' his true intentions to deceive the world. Christians, God willing, will recognize and resist him. However, a rebellious world, that has already rejected the truth, will be deceived.

According to the working of Satan… (2 Thessalonians 2:9)

In order that Satan might not outwit us.
For we are not unaware of his schemes...
2 Corinthians 2:11

- Satan is clever and cunning. *Now the snake was more crafty...* (Genesis 3:1)
- Satan seeks to subvert God's authority. *Did God really say?* (Genesis 3:1)
- Satan seeks to liberate from God's authority. *Did God really say, "You must not..."* (Genesis 3:1)
- Satan seeks to appear to be helpful. *You will be as gods* (Genesis 3:4)
- Satan seeks to be seen to be concerned for man's physical needs. *Tell these stones to become bread* (Matthew 4:3)
- Satan seeks to be seen to be fair, exposing injustice. *You shall not die... for God knows...*(Genesis 3:4)
- Satan seeks to be seen to be generous. *I will give you all the kingdoms of the world* (Matthew 4:8)
- Satan seeks to replace God as the focus of Man's worship... *Fall down and worship me* (Matthew 4:8)
- Just because it tastes good, looks good and sounds good doesn't mean it is good.... *When the woman saw that the fruit of the tree was good for food and pleasing to the eye, and also desirable for gaining wisdom, she took some and ate it.* (Genesis 3:6)

The Anti-Christ: Public Speaker

The horn had eyes like the eyes of a human being
and a mouth that spoke boastfully.
Daniel 7:8

Public speaking or oratory is a powerful force. Ever since Marc Anthony expertly swayed the Roman crowd at Caesar's funeral in Shakespeare's classic Julius Caesar, leaders have recognised the force of words to persuade and manipulate a crowd or population. Hitler militarised an entire nation through the force of his oratory. In recent years Tony Blair, a lawyer by training, took Britain to war in Iraq with the turn of phrase, '*We are going to war to make peace.*'

Scriptures indicate that one of the Anti-Christ's characteristics will be his speech, the force of his words and oratory.

In Revelation chapters 13-19 we read of a man called *the beast*. He demands and receives worship (Rev 13:8), and is destroyed by the coming of Jesus (Rev 19:20). This matches him definitively with the Anti-Christ, the *man of sin* that we read of in 2 Thessalonians 2.

The dragon (Satan) gave the beast his power
and his throne and great authority. *(1)*
The beast was given a mouth *(2)* ***to utter proud words and blasphemies***
and ***to exercise its authority for forty-two months.****(3)*
It opened its mouth to blaspheme God*, and to slander his name*
and his dwelling place and those who live in heaven (4) ***It was given power***
to wage war against God's holy people and to conquer them *(5).* ***And it***

was given authority over every tribe, people, language and nation *(6). All inhabitants of the earth will worship the beast – all whose names have not been written in the Lamb's book of life (7).*

Revelation 13: 2b, 5-8

From this passage, we can glean the following information about the Anti-Christ or 'beast'.

1. He is Satanic
2. He will be a good speaker or orator.
3. He will be permitted to exercise authority for 42 months (three-and-a-half years)
4. He will speak against God, Heaven and the angels.
5. He will wage war against 'God's holy people', the church.
6. He will be given authority over the whole world, *over every tribe, people, language and nation.*
7. All the unsaved will worship him.

The talking *image of the beast* of Revelation 13 will be a wonder in this media-saturated age. Billions will tune in to listen to his speeches, in which he will paint a bright picture of the possibilities of his 'brave new world', while blaspheming God, heaven and the angels. The Scripture forewarns us that the unbelieving world won't be able to resist his satanic wisdom and will worship him.

Nothing is so unbelievable that oratory cannot make it acceptable.

Cicero

The Anti-Christ: The Kicker

Kicker : an unwelcome and unexpected turn of events.

> *It also forced all people, great and small, rich and poor, free and slave,*
> *to receive a mark on their right hands or on their foreheads*
> *so that they could not buy or sell unless they had the mark,*
> *which is the name of the beast or the number of its name.*
> **Revelation 13:16-17**

On Sunday afternoon September 14, 2008 Mohammed El-Erian, the CEO of PIMCO, California made a call to his wife. PIMCO was and still is one of the largest institutional investors in the USA. At that time it had over one trillion dollars under management. El-Erian told his wife to go to the ATM and draw cash, saying, "*I am not sure if the banks are going to open tomorrow.*" He comments, "*There was a feeling that the system was incredibly fragile and that the unthinkable was clearly thinkable.*" (Documentary 'Meltdown: The Secret History of the Global Economic Collapse'.) The term 'economic armageddon' was coined by commentators that weekend as Lehman Brothers Bank, UK$613 billion in debt, went bankrupt.

Meltdown was averted when the United States Government borrowed 700 billion dollars from local and foreign lenders to give to other troubled banks. Within two months, on November 26, the United States Federal Reserve initiated a plan that would eventually see it print a staggering US$ 1.7 trillion of new money, effectively giving it to banks as a bail out. The money printing plan became known as ‘quantitative easing.’ In the weeks and months to come, central banks around the world, from Britain, China and Dubai to Japan, followed suit with their own money printing and bail out schemes. Such money printing has previously been associated with the collapse of the Zimbabwean dollar in the early 2000’s and the German mark in the 1920’s. High school economics lessons teach us that money printing to pay debts leads to hyperinflation and the eventual collapse of the currency.

The economic system, that has made life comfortable for so many in the developed world, is in a very fragile state. Revelation 13:16-18 tells us that one day ‘the beast’ or Anti-Christ will introduce a new system, based around a consumer ‘mark’, with which people will buy and sell.

It also forced all people, great and small, rich and poor, free and slave (2),
to receive a mark on their right hands or on their foreheads (1),
so that they could not buy or sell unless they had the mark (3),
which is the name of the beast or the number of its name.
This calls for wisdom. Let the person who has insight calculate
the number of the beast, for it is the number of a man. That number is 666.

Revelation 13:16-18

Points from this passage:

1. A compulsory ‘*mark*’ will be introduced.
2. It will be for *all* (verse 13).
3. People without the ‘*mark*’ will not be able to buy or sell.
4. The mark and the Anti-Christ have a related number, 666.

In Revelation 14 we read of the consequences of receiving this mark.

> *If anyone worships the beast and its image and receives its mark on their forehead or on their hand, they, too, will drink the wine of God's fury, which has been poured full strength into the cup of his wrath.*
> **Revelation 14:9**

The technology for such a mark is available today. We are familiar with the chip-and-pin technology that is used on credit cards. To take that a step further, human chip implants are being trialled and the advantages advertised.

A BBC article * opens with these words:

"*With a chip under your skin, you can do everything from unlocking doors to starting motorbikes*," says Rank Swain, who has been trying to get his own implant. The journalist closes by saying:

"*It marks the beginnings of a slow move toward a world where everything will be accessed from a single RFID microchip. If that day comes, I can't think of a safer place to keep it than inside my own body.*"

This is the kicker to the Anti-Christ's programme. While promising peace, freedom and liberty for all, he will enslave the world through his mark.

This new system will make it impossible for Christians throughout the world to continue in their accustomed lifestyles. Forbidden by Scripture to take the mark, and therefore unable to buy or sell, Christians will have to depend wholly on the Father for provision.

Now that's really a kicker.

The Anti-Christ: Hubris

And the God of peace shall bruise Satan under your feet shortly.
Romans 16:20 (KJV)

In Greek tragedy hubris was pride towards and in defiance of the Gods, that was in itself its own nemesis. Nowadays it relates to the downfall of an individual, due to excessive arrogance.

The Anti-Christ having aspired to be God himself will suffer the greatest fall of them all. His end is decreed in Daniel 9:27 and described in Daniel chapters 7 and 8, 2 Thessalonians 2 and Revelation 19.

Until ***the end that is decreed is poured out on him***
Daniel 9:27

(He will) take his stand against the Prince of princes (Jesus),
yet he will be destroyed but not by human power.
Daniel 8:25

He will speak against the Most High and oppress his holy people...
But then the court will sit ***and his power will be taken away***
and completely destroyed forever.
Daniel 7:23, 25

And then the lawless one (Anti-Christ) will be revealed, ***whom the Lord Jesus will overthrow with the breath of his mouth and destroy by the splendour of his coming.***
2 Thessalonians 2:8

And I saw the beast, and the kings of the earth, and their armies, gathered together to wage war against the rider on the horse and his army. ***But the beast was captured and ... thrown alive into the fiery lake of burning sulphur.***
Revelation 19:20

Therefore, as we consider this fearsome figure let us remember he is, to all intents and purposes, already defeated. His arrogance and defiance of God, his hubris, will be his downfall, defeated not by human power, but by Jesus himself.

The words of Martin Luther, who knew all about defying powerful authoritarian figures, encourages us to face this landmark figure with courage.

And though this world, with devils filled, should threaten to undo us,
we will not fear, for God hath willed his truth to triumph through us.
The Prince of Darkness grim, we tremble not for him;
his rage we can endure, for lo, his doom is sure; one little word shall fell him.
Martin Luther
Excerpt from: *A Mighty Fortress Is Our God*

Pause

Once again, I would suggest that you pause to digest some of this information before moving on. Re-read the Scriptures yourself, internalising the truth that they communicate. Please, do also take some time to be refreshed by reading other devotional material. This will renew a faith-filled, heavenly perspective.

We now move on to look in greater detail at the great tribulation that will take place after the Anti-Christ sets up the abomination of desolation.

Summary of Chapter 7

The Anti-Christ

1. He is a ruler related in some way to Rome or Europe, who will set up 'the abomination of desolation'. (Daniel 9:26-27)
2. He will rise in a time of rebellion or falling away from God.
3. Jesus cannot come back until this man is revealed.
4. He will oppose God; sit in the Temple, claiming to be God himself.
5. He will be defeated and destroyed by the Second Coming of Jesus.
6. He will act in accordance to the way Satan works.
7. He will display power through signs and wonders.

8. The unsaved, having rejected the truth, will be deceived. He is Satanic. (2 Thessalonians 2:1-10)
9. He will be a speaker or orator.
10. He will exercise authority for 42 months.
11. He will speak against God, heaven and the angels.
12. He will wage war against 'God's holy people', the church.
13. He will be given authority over the whole world.
14. All the unsaved will worship him. (Revelation 13:2,5-8)
15. A compulsory 'mark' will be introduced.
16. It will be for 'all'.
17. People without the 'mark' won't be able to buy or sell.
18. The mark and the Anti Christ have a related number, 666. (Revelation 13:16-18).
19. His end is decreed (Daniel 9:27)
20. He will be defeated, not by man but by the returning Christ. (2 Thessalonians 2:8)
21. He will be destroyed in a lake of fire. (Revelation 19:20)

Chapter 8

The Great Tribulation

For then shall be great tribulation,
such as was not since the beginning of the world to this time,
no, nor ever shall be...
Matthew 24:21 (KJV)

The Tribulation

His bride has made herself ready.

Revelation 19:7

The word tribulation has its root in the Latin word *tribulum,* used to describe a Roman threshing tool for separating mature grain from its chaff. A helpful explanation concerning threshing in Scripture comes from George D Watson, a late nineteenth century preacher.

There are several references in the Scripture to threshing out chaff. Even though God wants it removed, chaff is not a type of sin. It is essential to the growing of grain. Except for the chaff, a grain of wheat would be lost in its early stage of development. However, it only serves a temporary purpose. When the chaff is no longer needed, it must be removed.

The *tribulum* therefore played a key role in removing chaff prior to bringing in the grain. It didn't damage the grain. It transformed it and prepared it for the storehouse. This time of tribulation before Jesus' return will serve a similarly useful purpose for the church, removing unnecessary 'chaff' from our lives, so we are ready to meet with Him.

Many of us have gone through difficult experiences in which we have shed 'chaff'. Though trying, these experiences ultimately brought out the life of Christ in us. Looking back, we see them as valuable times. By understanding God's purposes for tribulation, we can redeem it. Instead of just looking at it as a wearying and worrying time of trouble, the church can look forward to being transformed through it, made ready for Christ's return.

Flight

For then shall be great tribulation…… Then let those who are in Judea flee to the mountains.
Matthew 24:15, 16 (NKJV)

It's every family's worst nightmare: to be forced to leave one's home, one's work and one's friends on short notice with little hope of ever returning. Over 300,000 Syrians have left their homes as a result of the current civil war. Many made perilous journeys across land and sea, seeking refuge in Europe.

The most famous Biblical flight was the Exodus. Millions of Israelites left their homes of 400 years to journey towards the Promised Lane. During their flight they faced times of great testing, pursued by Pharaoh's army and travelling in the wilderness for forty years. However, they also experienced an amazing series of miracles and deliverances as God faithfully led and cared for them day by day.

Jesus advises us that when the abomination is set up and the time of tribulation begins, it will once again be time to flee.

Then let those who are in Judea flee to the mountains. *Let him who is on the housetop not go down to take anything out of the house. Let him who is in the field not go back to get his clothes.*

But woe to those who are pregnant women and to those who are nursing babies in those days. And pray that your flight may not be in winter or on the Sabbath.
For then shall be great tribulation
Matthew 24: 16-21

Although His advice is to those in Judea, the circumstances may well dictate that this applies worldwide. A new world leader will have risen, demanding worship and given authority over the whole world, *over every tribe, people, language and nation* (Revelation 13:7). A new economic system will have been introduced with a compulsory mark that Christians are forbidden to take. Jesus' warning, therefore, to take flight seems sensible.

Like the children of Israel, Christians will have much to anticipate. The promised land of Jesus' return will be reached *immediately after the tribulation of those days* (Mat 24:31). So, although we will be sad to leave our homes, we will be journeying towards a glorious destination. However, like the children of Israel, our flight will test our faith and dependence on God like never before.

The Wilderness

The women fled into the wilderness to a place prepared for her by God, where she might be taken care of for 1,260 days.
Revelation 12:6

The women was given the two wings of a great eagle, so that she might fly to the place prepared for her in the wilderness, where she would be taken care of for a time, times and half a time, out of the serpent's reach.

Revelation 12:14

Don't you just love the wilderness? In the British Isles there are areas of outstanding beauty; the Brecon Beacons, the Lake District and the Highlands of Scotland. They are wonderfully undisturbed and undeveloped areas, where we can unwind and be refreshed. There is something so liberating about leaving human civilisation behind and being thoroughly submerged in the God-created nature of the wilderness.

In Revelation 12, found in full in the appendix, we read of a woman and a dragon. This woman has brought forth a man child (Jesus) who will rule all nations with a rod of iron (Rev 12:1-5). We identify the woman as God's people on earth, the church. The dragon, named in the text as Satan, is cast out of Heaven, and makes war with the woman and the rest of her offspring (believers) (Rev 12:9-13).

In Matthew 24 Jesus advises Christians to flee. In Revelation 12 verses 6 and 14, Christians are told where to flee. John tells us that God will prepare a place in the wilderness where He will take care of the church during the time to tribulation.

In verse 14 we read that the woman will be

*........given **two wings of a great eagle**, so that she might fly to the place prepared for her in the wilderness.*

The *two wings of a great eagle* may be an indication that Christians will use air travel to get to these wilderness places. After all, if John saw air travel in his vision in Revelation, *wings of a great eagle* would be a fair, and perhaps his only, means of describing it.

This isn't the first time that God will have brought his children into the wilderness. There are several examples in Scripture.

God led and fed Moses and the children of Israel in the wilderness for forty years. This encourages us that He will once again guide and provide for his people during this tribulation period as He promises in His Word.

These Scriptures in Revelation state that the church won't be in the wilderness for the forty years that the children of Israel endured. They are explicit that this time will last *1,260 days* (verse 6) or *a times and times and half a time* (verse 14). The latter is a time frame, repeated in Daniel chapters 7 and 12, that represents three-and-a-half years. (A time (1) and times (2) and half a time (1/2) = 3 ½ years). 3 ½ years equates to 1,260 days. The two verses speak of the same time period. (We will look at this in more detail in the next section.)

We can also remind ourselves how God sent ravens to bring bread and meat for Elijah by the brook Cherith. When the brook ran dry, God guided Elijah to the widow of Zarepath whose jar of flour and cruise of oil miraculously remained full. In a foreshadowing of the future time of great tribulation, Elijah's stay in the wilderness was also for three-and-a-half-years.

> *Elijah was a human being, even as we are. He prayed earnestly that it would not rain, and it did not rain on the land for three-and-a-half years.*

Again he prayed, and the heavens gave rain,
and the earth produced its crops.
James 5: 17-18

These Bible stories are markers of God's care for His children in times of great difficulty. In light of them, we can trust the Revelation Scriptures that tell us that God has planned an excursion into the wilderness for His children during the tribulation. Looking at His faithfulness in the past encourages us that His Word is reliable for this future time.

Times and Seasons

1,260 days...a time and times and half a time..
Rev 12:6,14

At the beginning of our family drive to Wales my mother would turn to us three boys, and say, "I don't know what time we will arrive at the cottage, however I can tell you that once we pass the village shop, we will be there in fifteen minutes." At the point of departure, she didn't know the time we would arrive. However, she was able to make a prediction in relation to the last landmark we would pass.

This is also what Scripture seems to do, when it gives a particular limit to the time in the wilderness. We don't know the day or the hour when Jesus will return, but we do know from the Scripture that the time of tribulation is limited (Matthew 24:22).

The woman fled into the wilderness to a place prepared for her by God, where she might be taken care of for ***1,260 days.***

Revelation 12:6

The woman was given the two wings of a great eagle, so that she might fly to the place prepared for her in the wilderness, where she would be take care of for a ***time, times and half a time****, out of the serpent's reach.*

Revelation 12:14

This same time period is repeated in many other passages relating to the last days. If you do the maths, you will find that 42 months, 1260 days and 3 and a half years are equal time periods.

They will trample on the holy city for ***42 months****. And I will appoint my two witnesses, and they will prophesy for* ***1,260 days****, clothed in sackcloth.*

Revelation 11:2-3

The beast was given a mouth to utter proud words and blasphemies and to exercise its authority ***for forty-two months.***

Revelation 13:5

He will speak against the Most High and oppress His holy people and try to change the set times and the laws. The holy people will be delivered into his hands for ***a time, times and half a time****.*

Daniel 7:25

It will be for ***a time, times and half a time****, when the power of the holy* *people has been finally broken; all these things will be completed.*

Daniel 12:7

The end of the last seven years of Gabriel's decree in Daniel 9 takes place three-and-a-half years after the abomination is set up.

In the middle of the 'seven' *he will put an end to sacrifice and offering. And at the temple he will set up an abomination that causes desolation, until the end that is decreed is poured out on him.*

Daniel 9:27

When a particular time period is repeated ***eight*** times in Scripture we should pay attention! God is hammering on this particular nail many times throughout Scripture to encourage us that this difficult, trouble-filled time will be limited or *shortened,* as Jesus says in Matthew 24.

And except those days should be shortened, there should no flesh be saved: but for the elect's sake ***those days shall be shortened.***

Matthew 24:22 (KJV)

Jesus encourages us that immediately after the tribulation of those days, He will return (Matthew 24: 29, 31). Therefore, the beginning of the tribulation will be similar to the ringing of the bell for the last lap of a 3,000 metre steeplechase. When they hear the ring of the bell, tired runners know exactly how much further they have to run and can pace themselves as they strain towards the finishing line.

In the same way when we enter the time of tribulation, the 'bell' will be rung and the countdown to Christ's return will begin. The finishing line will be in sight and we will strain towards it, knowing that the darkness and trying times will soon be transformed by the return of Christ.

This is a sign of God's love for us, His children. He understands that such a time would be impossible to bear unless we knew that it is limited to a specific time frame.

We can now complete a diagram of Daniel 9's final seven year period.

The Final 'Seven' or Seven Year Period of Daniel 9

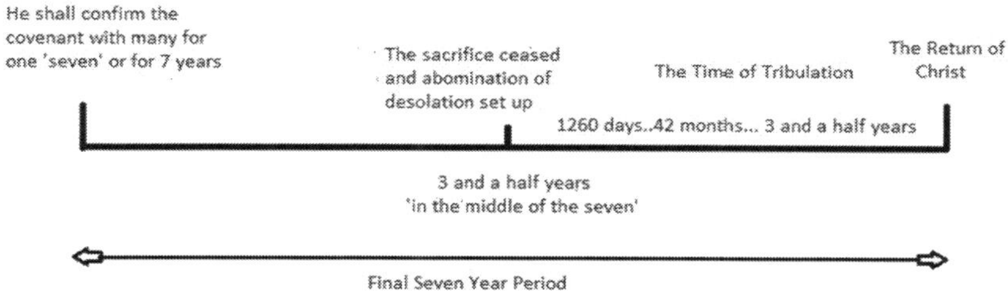

My mother couldn't predict the time we would arrive at our cottage in Wales as we left London. However, she could tell us exactly when we would arrive once we had passed the local village shop. Similarly, Jesus couldn't tell his disciples the day or the hour in Matthew 24. However, the congruent Scriptural evidence in Daniel and Revelation cannot be ignored. We have been given definite information about the length of rule of the Anti-Christ and the time of tribulation. The Anti-Christ's rule is limited by Scripture to forty-two months or three-and-a-half years and this is the exact period that God promises to look after His church in Revelation 12. Jesus promises to return 'immediately' after this tribulation period.

Thank God for giving us this foreknowledge that will sustain the church during the time of tribulation.

Victory out of Defeat

Who will separate us from the love of Christ?
Shall trouble or hardship or persecution or famine
or nakedness or danger or sword?
As it is written; "For your sake we face death all day long;
we are considered as sheep to be slaughtered."
No, in all these things we are more than conquerors through him who loved us.
Romans 8: 35-37

The disciples scattered. Peter, distraught, returned to his fishing boat. It had all ended in disaster, apparently. All hopes had been dashed, all dreams broken. Their leader had been taken and summarily executed. The euphoria of Palm Sunday had evaporated into hopelessness and despair. What had gone wrong? How could they have been so hopelessly mistaken?

After three days, Christ's resurrection demonstrated that nothing had gone wrong. Instead, it dawned on the disciples that this painful process had been part of God's plan all along. The Romans and Pharisees hadn't taken Jesus' life, but He had laid it down voluntarily for a greater and more glorious eternal victory. Eventually, the disciples could glory in this seeming defeat as the day of Pentecost arrived and they were all possessed by the presence of God, more effective even than the singular presence of Jesus.

The tribulation period will also appear to be a lost cause. The Scriptures speak of defeat.

He will speak against the Most High and oppress his holy people and try to change the set times and the laws. ***The holy people will be delivered into his hands*** *for a time, times and half a time.*

Daniel 7:25

He will destroy those who are mighty, the holy people.

Daniel 8:24

Then the dragon was enraged at the woman and ***went off to wage war against the rest of her offspring*** *– those who keep God's commands and hold fast their testimony about Jesus.*

Revelation 12:17

It (the beast) was given power to wage war against God's holy people and to conquer them.

Revelation 13:7

It sounds like defeat, doesn't it? The saints aren't given authority over the Anti-Christ, but to the contrary, he is given physical authority over them. Where's the victory in that?

In reality, however, just as Jesus conquered the devil on the cross, Scriptures tell us that Christians will conquer Satan during the tribulation.

They triumphed over him by the blood of the Lamb and by the word of their testimony*; they did not love their lives so much as to shrink from death.*

Revelation 12:11

We will triumph through testifying of our faith in the cross and resurrection that removes the sting of death and the victory of the grave.

As Jesus rose in victory from the grave to a heavenly throne, the Scriptures indicated martyred Christians will rise to rule and reign with Christ shortly after the time of tribulation.

And I saw the souls of those who had been beheaded because of
their testimony about Jesus and because of the word of God.
They had not worshiped the beast or its image
and had not received its mark on their foreheads or their hands.
They came to life and reigned with Christ a thousand years.

Revelation 20:4

Christians who are filled with His Spirit will resist the Anti-Christ's rule and teach many others the appropriate Scriptures. We read in Revelation 11 of two 'witnesses' who testify for the entire three-and-a-half years of tribulation (Revelation 11:3-13). It won't be all gloom and doom. God will show himself strong on behalf of those whose hearts are filled with Him.

But the people that do know their God shall be strong, and do exploits. And they that understand among the people shall instruct many:
Daniel 11: 32b (KJV).

Christians will rise up, teaching and testifying and opposing the Anti-Christ's teachings and practices. New heroes of the faith will appear, filled with grace and truth, their names to be etched in history alongside the ancient heroes of Hebrews 11. Exploits will be recorded that will reverberate through eternity. This is what we as believers can aspire to; to know our God, be strong, to understand and teach others.

The Scriptures in this section demonstrate that though the Anti-Christ is given authority over the church as a whole, those who are filled with a knowledge of God will demonstrate His power and faithfulness to the world. They will be rewarded greatly at Christ's return, which will take place immediately after the tribulation period.

Babylon The Great

"I sit enthroned as queen. I am not a widow; I will never mourn."
Revelation 18:7

Repentance is a key step to becoming a Christian. For many years I thought that I could make it through life on my own. I saw no need to repent. I had fanciful dreams about who I was and lived a life of outward confidence. However, the day came that I looked at myself in the mirror and realised I needed something outside of myself to save me. Like the Titanic with a fatal hole below the water line, I recognised I was doomed to sink without salvation. That moment of recognising my sin within and repenting, fundamentally changed my life and set me on the road of walking with Christ.

There is one last great character in Last Days' Scripture and the tribulation period.. In Revelation 17, 18 and 19, we read of a final world power that won't repent and therefore experiences the judgement of God before the return of Christ. I have summarised the chapters below, however, please do read them in full in the appendix. Familiarise yourself with them, and highlight the key verses.

This power is graphically depicted as a wealthy woman. She thinks she is a queen (18:7) but God calls her Babylon, the Prostitute (17:5). She holds a golden cup full of adulteries (17:4), and rules over the kings of the earth (17:18). She has become excessively rich as a great trader and consumer (17:4, 18:3), committing adultery with the kings and merchants of the world (18: 3, 9). She has 'fallen' and become possessed by demons (18:2). The language of adultery suggests that this woman was once 'married' to Christ; in other words, was once a Christian nation.

She is violent, guilty of many crimes, responsible for much slaughter and the blood of many of God's children (17:6; 18:24). She is full of deceit (18:23). Because she is proud, boastful and will not repent (18:7), God will put it in the hearts of ten kings, allies of the Anti-

Christ beast, to utterly burn her with fire (17:12, 16-17). She will be totally devastated and destroyed in one hour (18:10, 17). The Heavens give a shout of praise at this judgement (19: 1-2). God calls His people who inhabit her to come out, so that they won't share in this judgement (18: 4-5)

This woman sits on seven hills (17:9). This appears to be a reference to Rome, which was built on seven hills. Many commentators have therefore identified this graphic figure as Rome or the Catholic Church. In their time, both Rome and the Catholic Church were wealthy, corrupted, violent and powerful. However, they don't rule over the kings of the earth in the present as they did in the past. Therefore, it may be wise for Christendom as a whole, which grew out of Rome and the Catholic Church, to reflect on this text.

There are wealthy Christian countries that exert a great deal of power in the world today. However, discernment is needed to determine to what extent their actions reflect or contradict Christian values. It isn't what they say that counts, but what they do. What are the 'fruits' (Matthew 7:16) seen both in their societies at home, and the results of their foreign policies abroad? Babylon does not look in the mirror to see what she has become. She refuses to see either the corruption within or the effects of her actions on other nations. She becomes her own worst enemy, deceiving herself and the world around her. Christ followers cannot afford to ignore these passages. They must take a long and possibly painful look in the mirror. May God's spirit give us all wisdom in discerning this mystery.

Jesus will return to defeat the Anti-Christ's regime, but first He will allow it to wreak judgement on the adulterous unrepentant Babylon the Great. Christians are warned to discern this mystery and '*come out of her*', to get out, at the appropriate time before the judgement falls.

After rejoicing over the judgement of Babylon in Revelation 19: 1-5, the Heavens prepare for the arrival of the bride of Christ, the church in Revelation 19: 6-8. This appears to place the judgement of Babylon towards the end of the time of tribulation. This is the seventh landmark we can add to our list.

Landmarks to be Passed before Christ's Return

1. Gospel Preached in all the World (Matthew 24:14)
2. Rebuilding of the Jewish Temple (Matthew 24:1; Daniel 9:27, 11:31)
3. The Confirming of a Holy Covenant for seven years (Daniel 9:27)
4. The Anti-Christ Revealed (2 Thessalonians 2: 3-8)
5. The Abomination of Desolation Set Up (Matthew 24:15-20; Daniel 9:27, 11:31)
6. The Time of Tribulation (Matthew 24:21-28; Daniel 12:1)
7. The Judgement of Babylon the Great (Revelation 17-18)
8. The Second coming of Jesus (Matthew 24: 29-30; Daniel 7:13; 2 Thessalonians 2:8)

Pause

We have now completed the detailed section of the book. Perhaps like Daniel you may feel you need a lie down! The scriptures have been weighty and disturbing. However, God's Word and His promises stand and He will bring us through these times of trouble. Encourage yourself in Him.

When you pass through the waters, I will be with you;
And through the rivers, they shall not overflow you.
When you walk through the fire, you shall not be burned,
Isaiah 43:2 (NKJV)

Summary of Chapter 8

The Tribulation

1. The time of Tribulation will prepare us to meet Jesus (Revelation 19:7)
2. He advises us to flee (Matthew 24: 16-21)
3. He will prepare a place for the church in the wilderness (Revelation 12:6;14)
4. The Tribulation will last three-and-a-half years (Revelation 13: 5; 12: 6,14)
5. The Anti-Christ will overwhelm the church (Revelation 13:7)
6. However, Spirit-filled Christians will still rise up in opposition (Daniel 11: 32-33)
7. 'Babylon the Great' will be punished. Christians are warned to 'come out of her' (Revelation 17-19)
8. Jesus will return immediately after the time of tribulation. (Matthew 24:29)

Conclusion

We also have the prophetic message as something completely reliable,
and you will do well to pay attention to it,
until the day dawns and the morning star rises in your hearts.
2 Peter 1:19

We've taken a whistle stop tour through Scripture, and have discovered seven major landmarks that will be passed before Christ's return. I trust you will have considered this tour worthwhile and that, despite the seriousness of the topic, the Word of God will have ministered life and light to you.

This is a traveller's guide in which we've looked at the major landmarks. First time tourists visiting London focus on the major attractions of Big Ben, Trafalgar Square and Houses of Parliament. So, it's entirely right that first time visitors of Last Days' Scripture should initially spend their time examining the Abomination of Desolation, the Anti-Christ and the Time of Tribulation. These are the major landmarks that Jesus and Scripture refer us to.

Reading the passages concerning the Abomination of Desolation, the Anti-Christ, the Great Tribulation and Christ's Return has helped us to build a structure of Scriptural knowledge, with the words of Jesus as the foundation. Other Scriptures can be incorporated into this structure if they don't contradict or weaken it. The sure Word of Scripture testifies to these landmarks. So, don't be intimidated by the arguments of others; to the contrary, own the Scriptures yourself. Stand on the foundational narratives of Matthew 24 and 2 Thessalonians 2 and don't be moved away from them.

In 2 Peter 1:19, Peter describes the Word of God as *completely reliable*. I pray you are able, as Peter suggests, to *pay attention to it* and *do well*. God will prepare you, as you wait to recognize and pass the scriptural landmarks.

Review of The Landmarks to be Passed before Christ's Return

1. Gospel Preached in all the World (Matthew 24:14)
2. Rebuilding of the Jewish Temple (Matthew 24:15; Daniel 9:27; 11:31)
3. The Confirming of a Holy Covenant for seven years (Daniel 9:27)
4. The Anti-Christ Revealed (2 Thessalonians 2: 3-8)
5. Abomination of Desolation Set Up (Matthew 24: 15-20; Daniel 9:27, 11:31.)
6. The Time of Tribulation (Matthew 24:15-20: Daniel 9:27; 11:31)
7. The Judgement of Babylon (Revelation 17 – 19)
8. The Second Coming of Jesus (Matthew 24: 29-30; Daniel 7:13; 1 Thessalonians 4: 16-18; 2 Thessalonians 2:8)

Reflection

In the classic seventeenth century allegorical novel, *Pilgrim's Progress,* Christian reads in a book that his home city is in danger of judgement and destruction. The book also convicts him of his own sin, manifesting itself as a heavy burden on his back. After an encounter with a man called Evangelist, he decides to leave his home city, the city of destruction, and embark on a journey towards the Celestial City.

Christian passes through the *bog of discouragement,* climbs the *hill of difficulty* and finally and joyously loses his burden at the foot of the cross. He faces persecution in the *market place of Vanity Fair.* He walks with and enjoys wonderful fellowship with three companions, Faithful, Help and Hopeful and is equipped with godly armour by three sisters, name Charity, Prudence and Piety. After many adventures, he and Hopeful arrive at the Celestial City. Angels usher them through the gates where they are greeted with rejoicing and singing. They are given harps to praise and crowns for their honour, as they hear the words "*Enter into the joy of the Lord.*" His wife and children follow soon after, making Christian eternally grateful that he had made the decision to leave the city of destruction.

I pray that you, like Christian, will recognise the brokenness of the present world we live in and that it is passing away; and that you too will be encouraged to step out on a new journey towards God's eternal kingdom. You can do this by putting your trust in Christ, surrendering your life to Him, and embracing the ways and values of His Spirit and His Kingdom. You have His Word and the

Holy Spirit as your guides and fellow Christians as your companions. It's the greatest adventure of all.

Please do not be troubled by what we have read. If Jesus tells us not to be troubled, then there must be just cause not to be troubled. That just cause is, and always will be, in Him, through Him and with Him.

Prayer:

Lord Jesus I thank you for Your Word, which sheds light on the path ahead. I trust You, that You are my Good Shepherd. The safest place in troubling times is in You and in Your care. Please give me peace in the knowledge that You love me and care for me. In light of Your Word, I surrender to You Lord Jesus and put my life into Your hands.

Please fill me with your Holy Spirit so that I can fully know You and Your will for my life. Please give me great love and wisdom as I reassess my life and pray how I can step out anew to follow You.

Please open doors for me to bless others with the Good News of Your love. May I be Your voice to encourage, Your hands to support, help and heal, and Your feet, willing to go into the world and proclaim Your name.

In Jesus Name. Amen

I recommend two books by Mark Batterson, pastor of National Community Church, Washington. *Wild Goose Chase* and *In a Pit with a Lion on a Snowy Day* will encourage you as you step out and embrace the Spirit-filled journey that Jesus has planned for you.

Wild at Heart by John Eldredge describes man's deep desires for challenge, risk and adventure. These desires will be fully met as Christians navigate their way through the last days' landmarks to Christ's return.

My desire is that you and I won't have to go through these times. I am enjoying myself too much in Gospel living and work to wish that the darkness fall around me in my lifetime. However, if it does, I trust that God, through His Word and Spirit, will help me to be ready and equipped for it.

God's blessings on your life, God's peace and courage in your heart, and God's speed on your journey.

Summaries for Quick Referencing

Chapter 1

Are We Looking Forwards Clearly?

1. We should look forwards to Jesus' Second Coming as well as looking backwards at the cross (Philippians 3:13).
2. We should pray for a Spirit-filled discernment *of* the Scriptures and a Spirit-filled response *to* the Scriptures (Matthew 16:3).
3. The supreme authority of the words of Jesus make them the best place to start building our theology (Matthew 24:35).

Chapter 2

The Landmarks of Matthew Chapter 24

1. God's Word will provide us with a refuge of faith and certainty in tumultuous times when false prophets will abound. (Matthew 24: 5,11,24)
2. God's Word indicates a testing time before Jesus' return. Being prepared, like a woman preparing for giving birth, will greatly improve the church's ability to respond. (Matthew 24:7)
3. Jesus can't come back 'any time'. Jesus, in Matthew 24, and Paul,

in 2 Thessalonians 2, give us landmarks that must be passed before Jesus returns:

1. Gospel Preached in All the World (Matthew 24:14)
2. The Anti-Christ Revealed (2Thessalonians 2: 6-8)
3. Abomination of Desolation (Matthew 24:15-20)
4. Time of Tribulation (Matthew 24: 21-29)
5. Second Coming of Christ (Matthew 24:30-31)

We now have a foundation for our end time theology. We can call into question interpretations and doctrines that do not align with the parameters laid out in Matthew 24.

4. Let's be cautions and wise about how we handle the Scriptures knowing that, like the mountains in the distance on a long drive, appearances can be deceptive. Let's therefore avoid unwise predications and conjectures. Let's rather stick to Scripture in our teachings and discussions. (Luke 21:19)
5. The narrative of Matthew 24 tells us God's story will end with a memorable and tension filled finale. (Matthew 24:15-29)
6. Staying simple, trusting His word, avoids confusion. (2 Corinthians 11:3)

Chapter 3

Troubled?

1. Jesus warns that many will be troubled and offended. (Matthew 24:10)

2. Jesus warns us not to be troubled by last days' events (Matthew 24:6)
3. God will meet us at the level of our faith (Matthew 17:20)
4. God will meet us at the level of our ability (2 Corinthians 12:9)
5. It's His job to bring us through, not ours. The Lord will perfect that which concerns us. (Psalm 138:8)

Chapter 4

The Return of The King

1. Jesus returns immediately after the time of tribulation (Matthew 24:30-31)
2. The saved church, both dead and alive, will be gathered up by angels and meet Jesus in the air (1Thessalonians 4:16-18)
3. The saved church will then attend the wedding supper of the Lamb (Revelation 19:5)
4. And be rewarded at the judgement seat of Christ (2 Corinthians 5:10)
5. Jesus will then lead a heavenly invasion (Revelation 19: 11-20)
6. And start His thousand-year rule with the saints (Revelation 20:6)

Chapter 5

Preparations

1. Be ready for these times (Matthew 24:44)
2. Know and share the Word of God about these times (Matthew 24: 4, 45)
3. Be filled with the Spirit, surrendered to the Spirit, and learn how to be led by the Spirit (Matthew 25: 1-13)
4. Stay busy in Gospel living and work (Matthew 25:14-30)

Chapter 6

The Abomination of Desolation

1. The term abomination of desolation is found in Daniel 9:27.
2. It is part of Gabriel's seventy 'seven' decree that also includes the crucifixion of Christ and the destruction of the Jewish Temple in 70AD.

Q: Who sets up the abomination of desolation?

A: A 'ruler' related in some way to Rome or Europe. (Daniel 9:26,27)

Q: When is the abomination of desolation set up?

A: In the middle of a seven-year period after the signing or confirming of a covenant or treaty (Daniel 9:27).

Q: Where is the abomination of desolation set up?

A: Scripture points to it being in the Holy Place, the rebuilt Jerusalem Temple. (Matthew 24:15; Daniel 9:27, 11:31; 2 Thessalonians 2:3-4)

Q: What is the abomination of desolation?

A: It is something that is 'set up'; most likely to be the 'talking image' of a satanic world leader described in Revelations 13:14-15 and 2 Thessalonians 2:3-4.

Chapter 7

The Anti-Christ

1. He is a ruler related in some way to Rome or Europe, who will set up 'the abomination of desolation'. (Daniel 9:26-27)
2. He will rise in a time of rebellion or falling away from God.
3. Jesus cannot come back until this man is revealed. He will oppose God; sit in the Temple, claiming to be God himself.
4. He will be defeated and destroyed by the Second Coming of Jesus. He will act in accordance to the way Satan works.
5. He will display power through signs and wonders.
6. The unsaved, having rejected the truth, will be deceived. He is Satanic. (2 Thessalonians 2:1-10)
7. He will be a speaker or orator.
8. He will exercise authority for 42 months.
9. He will speak against God, heaven and the angels.
10. He will wage war against 'God's holy people', the church.

11. He will be given authority over the whole world.
12. All the unsaved will worship him. (Revelation 13:2,5-8)
13. A compulsory 'mark' will be introduced.
14. It will be for 'all'.
15. People without the 'mark' won't be able to buy or sell.
16. The mark and the Anti Christ have a related number, 666. (Revelation 13:16-18)
17. His end is decreed (Daniel 9:27)
18. He will be defeated, not by man but by the returning Christ. (2 Thessalonians 2:8)
19. He will be destroyed in the lake of fire. (Revelation 19:20)

Chapter 8

The Tribulation

1. The time of Tribulation will prepare us to meet Jesus (Revelation 19:7)
2. He advises us to flee (Matthew 24: 16-21)
3. He will prepare a place for the church in the wilderness (Revelation 12:6;14)
4. The Tribulation will last three-and-a-half years (Revelation 13: 5; 12: 6,14)
5. The Anti-Christ will overwhelm the church (Revelation 13:7)
6. However, Spirit-filled Christians will rise up in opposition (Daniel 11: 32-33)

7. 'Babylon the Great' will be punished. Christians are warned to 'come out of her' (Revelation 17-19) 8. Jesus will return immediately after the time of tribulation. Matthew 24:29)

Appendix

Matthew Chapter 24 (KJV)

24 And Jesus went out, and departed from the temple: and his disci-
ples came to him for to shew him the buildings of the temple. 2 And
Jesus said unto them, See ye not all these things? verily I say unto you,
There shall not be left here one stone upon another, that shall not be
thrown down.

3 And as he sat upon the mount of Olives, the disciples came unto
him privately, saying, Tell us, when shall these things be? and what
shall be the sign of thy coming, and of the end of the world?

4 And Jesus answered and said unto them, Take heed that no man
deceive you. 5 For many shall come in my name, saying, I am Christ; and
shall deceive many. 6 And ye shall hear of wars and rumours of wars:
see that ye be not troubled: for all these things must come to pass, but
the end is not yet. 7 For nation shall rise against nation, and kingdom
against kingdom: and there shall be famines, and pestilences, and
earthquakes, in divers places. 8 All these are the beginning of sorrows.

9 Then shall they deliver you up to be afflicted, and shall kill you:
and ye shall be hated of all nations for my name's sake. 10 And then
shall many be offended, and shall betray one another, and shall hate
one another. 11 And many false prophets shall rise, and shall deceive
many. 12 And because iniquity shall abound, the love of many shall
wax cold. 13 But he that shall endure unto the end, the same shall be

saved. [14] And this gospel of the kingdom shall be preached in all the world for a witness unto all nations; and then shall the end come.

[15] When ye therefore shall see the abomination of desolation, spoken of by Daniel the prophet, stand in the holy place, (whoso readeth, let him understand:) [16] Then let them which be in Judaea flee into the mountains:[17] Let him which is on the housetop not come down to take any thing out of his house:[18] Neither let him which is in the field return back to take his clothes.[19] And woe unto them that are with child, and to them that give suck in those days![20] But pray ye that your flight be not in the winter, neither on the sabbath day:

[21] For then shall be great tribulation, such as was not since the beginning of the world to this time, no, nor ever shall be.[22] And except those days should be shortened, there should no flesh be saved: but for the elect's sake those days shall be shortened.[23] Then if any man shall say unto you, Lo, here is Christ, or there; believe it not.[24] For there shall arise false Christs, and false prophets, and shall shew great signs and wonders; insomuch that, if it were possible, they shall deceive the very elect.[25] Behold, I have told you before.[26] Wherefore if they shall say unto you, Behold, he is in the desert; go not forth: behold, he is in the secret chambers; believe it not.[27] For as the lightning cometh out of the east, and shineth even unto the west; so shall also the coming of the Son of man be.[28] For wheresoever the carcase is, there will the eagles be gathered together.

[29] Immediately after the tribulation of those days shall the sun be darkened, and the moon shall not give her light, and the stars shall fall from heaven, and the powers of the heavens shall be shaken: [30] And then shall appear the sign of the Son of man in heaven: and

then shall all the tribes of the earth mourn, and they shall see the Son
of man coming in the clouds of heaven with power and great glory.
31 And he shall send his angels with a great sound of a trumpet, and
they shall gather together his elect from the four winds, from one end
of heaven to the other.

32 Now learn a parable of the fig tree; When his branch is yet ten-
der, and putteth forth leaves, ye know that summer is nigh: 33 So like-
wise ye, when ye shall see all these things, know that it is near, even at
the doors. 34 Verily I say unto you, This generation shall not pass, till
all these things be fulfilled. 35 Heaven and earth shall pass away, but
my words shall not pass away. 36 But of that day and hour knoweth no
man, no, not the angels of heaven, but my Father only.

37 But as the days of Noah were, so shall also the coming of the Son
of man be. 38 For as in the days that were before the flood they were
eating and drinking, marrying and giving in marriage, until the day
that Noe entered into the ark, 39 And knew not until the flood came,
and took them all away; so shall also the coming of the Son of man
be. 40 Then shall two be in the field; the one shall be taken, and the
other left. 41 Two women shall be grinding at the mill; the one shall
be taken, and the other left. 42 Watch therefore: for ye know not what
hour your Lord doth come.

43 But know this, that if the goodman of the house had known in
what watch the thief would come, he would have watched, and would
not have suffered his house to be broken up. 44 Therefore be ye also
ready: for in such an hour as ye think not the Son of man cometh.

45 Who then is a faithful and wise servant, whom his lord hath
made ruler over his household, to give them meat in due season?

46 Blessed is that servant, whom his lord when he cometh shall find so
doing. 47 Verily I say unto you, That he shall make him ruler over all
his goods. 48 But and if that evil servant shall say in his heart, My lord
delayeth his coming; 49 And shall begin to smite his fellow servants,
and to eat and drink with the drunken; 50 The lord of that servant shall
come in a day when he looketh not for him, and in an hour that he is
not aware of, 51 And shall cut him asunder, and appoint him his por-
tion with the hypocrites: there shall be weeping and gnashing of teeth.

Scriptures that speak of the signs of the times (TLB)

Matthew 24: 4-8 Jesus told them, "Don't let anyone fool you. For many will come claiming to be the Messiah and will lead many astray. When you hear of wars beginning, this does not signal my return; these must come, but the end is not yet. The nations and kingdoms of the earth will rise against each other, and there will be famines and earthquakes in many places. But all this will be only the beginning of the horrors to come.

2 Timothy 3: 1 – 4 You may as well know this too, Timothy, that in the last days it is going to be very difficult to be a Christian. For people will love only themselves and their money; they will be proud and boastful, sneering at God, disobedient to their parents, ungrateful to them, and thoroughly bad. They will be hard-headed and never give in to others; they will be constant liars and troublemakers and will think nothing of immorality. They will be rough and cruel, and sneer at those who try to be good. 4 They will betray their friends; they

will be hot headed, puffed up with pride, and prefer good times to worshiping God.

2 Thessalonians 2 For that day will not come until two things happen: first, there will be a time of great rebellion against God.

Daniel 12:4 "But Daniel, keep this prophecy a secret; seal it up so that it will not be understood until the end times, when travel and education shall be vastly increased!"

2 Peter 3: 3-5 First, I want to remind you that in the last days there will come scoffers who will do every wrong they can think of and laugh at the truth. This will be their line of argument: "So Jesus promised to come back, did he? Then where is he? He'll never come! Why, as far back as anyone can remember, everything has remained exactly as it was since the first day of creation.

Milk and Meat

> *Anyone who lives on milk, being still an infant is not acquainted with the teaching about righteousness. But solid food is for the mature, who by constant use have trained themselves to distinguish good from evil.*
>
> **Hebrews 5: 13-14**

In Hebrews 5, Paul differentiates between scriptural milk and scriptural solid food. The 'milk' can be read and understood by all, both new-born and mature Christians. It doesn't take much work. Like a glass of milk, you can just down it easily! However, solid food is like a juicy steak. It's challenging and requires a fair bit of chewing before it can be digested.

Paul says milk is for infants; solid food is for the mature. Some are reluctant to teach at all on the times that will precede the Second Coming, believing that their members 'are not ready for it', that it is too disturbing. This is understandable. Wisdom is needed for this topic. However, by withholding the 'solid food', leaders can unwittingly slow down and inhibit their congregations' ability to grow spiritually and properly distinguish '*good from evil*.'

AW Tozer wrote, "*The weakness of so many modern Christians is that they feel too much at home in the world.*" Instead of recognising that we are 'pilgrims and strangers' in this world, many of us feel 'at home', comfortable, secure and satisfied. The 'solid food' in these studies reveals the future of the world, that it will not be comfortable and secure. We recognise how temporary our earthly citizenship is and can then realign our priorities and invest more into the kingdom.

The studies in Daniel and Revelation are solid and meaty. Don't expect to chug them back like a glass of milk and move on. Some of the passages require time and work to be broken down and digested. However, they are also some of the most exciting Bible passages in Scripture, revealing God's sovereignty over all things.

The Seventy 'Sevens' of Daniel 9

Seventy 'sevens' are decreed for your people and your holy city...

Daniel 9:22-24

Throughout Bible history God has given His children prior knowledge of major events. He told Abraham how long the children of Israel would be in Egypt, 400 years (Genesis 15:13). He told Joseph via Pharaoh's dream about 14 years of Egyptian plenty and famine. God told Jeremiah that the captivity in Babylon would last 70 years. (Jeremiah 25:11-12, 29:10) In Daniel 4, Daniel decreed that Nebuchadnezzar would live seven humbling years as an animal. (Daniel 4:24-26)

Gabriel comes to Daniel with a specific timetable for the future of Israel and Jerusalem.

Seventy 'sevens' are decreed for your people and your holy city...

Daniel 9:22-24

Gabriel decreed seventy 'sevens' over Israel and Jerusalem. The word 'seven' is the Hebrew word 'shabua', meaning a seven-year period. (In Genesis 29:27 and 20, the word 'shabua' referred to the seven-year period that Jacob served Laban for his daughters.)

Gabriel's decree of seventy sevens therefore describes a period of 490 years (seventy x seven years).

The decree proclaims six events that will have taken place in Israel by the end of these 490 years.

...to finish transgression, to put an end to sin, to atone for wickedness, to bring in everlasting righteousness, to seal up vision and prophecy and to anoint the Most Holy Place.

Daniel 9:24

Without getting into a long theological discussion about these events, we are able conclude that the decree spans all the way to the Second Coming of Christ. We know this because it includes information about the abomination of desolation, which Jesus anchored close to His return in Matthew 24.

The Sixty-Nine 'Sevens'

> *Know and understand this: **From the time the word goes out to restore and rebuild Jerusalem until the Anointed One, the ruler comes**, there will be **seven 'sevens', and sixty-two 'sevens'**. It will be rebuilt with streets and a trench, but in times of trouble*[1].
>
> **Daniel 9:25**

Gabriel first announces a time span of ***seven 'sevens'*** and ***sixty-two 'sevens'***.

Seven 'sevens' (49 years) + sixty-two 'sevens' (434 years)
= Sixty-nine 'sevens' (49 + 434 = 483 years)

This is a period of 483 years.

This timespan begins with the order to '***restore and rebuild Jerusalem***' and ends with the '***Anointed One***' or Messiah.

The city of Jerusalem had been destroyed by the invasion of Nebuchadnezzar, but in 453 BC the order was given by Artaxerxes to

Nehemiah, permitting the Jews to rebuild the wall and the city of Jerusalem (Nehemiah 2:5)

453 BC + 483 years = 30 AD

If we add the 69 'sevens', 483 years, of the decree, to 453 BC, (the date ***the word went out to rebuild Jerusalem***), we see that Gabriel decreed 30AD as the date when '***the Anointed One***' Jesus would come.

Gabriel continues his decree:

After the sixty-two 'sevens', ***the Anointed One*** *will be put to death and will have nothing.*

Daniel 9:26

Gabriel decrees that Jesus, Messiah will be put to death, after the period of sixty-two sevens (30 AD!).

If Jesus was born in 4 BC, as historians believe, this decree, written over 500 years before, accurately announces the year of Jesus' crucifixion. Astounding! Only God himself could have made this decree through Gabriel. The first part of the decree has come to pass with astonishing accuracy! How were the religious leaders of Jesus' day ignorant of it! They crucified '***the Anointed One***', Jesus, despite God giving such a clear prophetic word to His people about the time of His arrival.

The Seventy Weeks of Daniel 9

The First 69 weeks

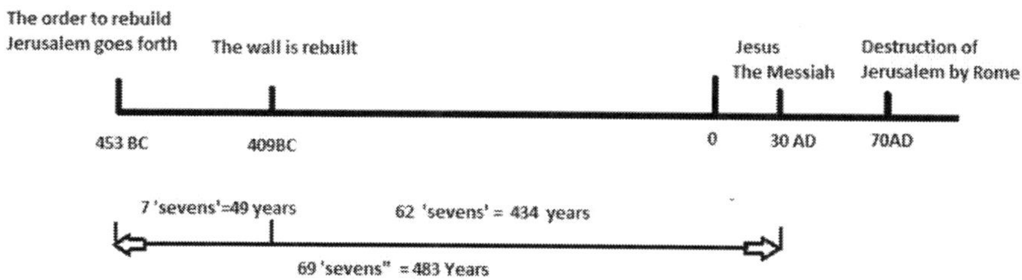

Following his prediction of this momentous event, Gabriel continues:

> *The people of the ruler* ***who will come*** *will destroy the city and the sanctuary. The end will come like a flood: War will continue until the end, and desolations have been decreed.*
>
> **Daniel 9:26**

In 70 AD Roman legions, sent to crush rebellion in Israel, destroyed the city and the Temple. '*The people of the ruler who will come*' are therefore the Romans or perhaps Europeans. They destroyed '*the city and the sanctuary*'.

At present, we do not know who this '*ruler who will come*' is. He features in the second part of the decree, which contains information about the abomination of desolation, tied by Jesus to occur soon before His return.

[1] (***'It will be rebuilt with streets and a trench, but in times of trou-***

ble' is a reference to the rebuilding of the wall of Jerusalem. It was rebuilt first in the first 'seven' 'sevens', or 49 years, in *times of trouble.* Nehemiah 4:17)

The 2030 Agenda for Sustainable Development

(The extract below is taken from a United Nations website)

The Global Goals have been introduced to the world

A 17 – point plan to end poverty, combat climate change and fight injustice and inequality

They are the biggest attempt in the history of the human race to make the world a better place. A plan that 193 governments have agreed, a plan that the world wants and needs, a plan backed by leading business and organisations, a to-do list for the planet that will only be achieved if everyone plays their part."

Transforming our world: the 2030 Agenda for Sustainable Development

Preamble

This Agenda is a plan of action for people, planet and prosperity. It also seeks to strengthen universal peace in larger freedom. We recognise that eradicating poverty in all its forms and dimensions, including extreme poverty, is the greatest global challenge and an indispensable requirement for sustainable development. All countries and all stakeholders, acting in collaborative partnership, will implement this plan. We are resolved to free the human race from the tyranny of poverty and want and to heal and secure our planet. We are determined to take the bold and transformative steps which are urgently needed to shift the world onto a sustainable and resilient path. As we embark on this collective journey, we pledge that no one will be left behind. The 17 Sustainable Development Goals and 169 targets which we are announcing today demonstrate the scale and ambition of this new universal Agenda. They seek to build on the Millennium Development Goals and complete what these did not achieve. They seek to realize the human rights of all and to achieve gender equality and the empowerment of all women and girls. They are integrated and indivisible and balance the three dimensions of sustainable development: the economic, social and environmental.

The Goals and targets will stimulate action over the next fifteen years in areas of critical importance for humanity and the planet:

People

We are determined to end poverty and hunger, in all their forms and dimensions, and to ensure that all human beings can fulfil their potential in dignity and equality and in a healthy environment.

Planet

We are determined to protect the planet from degradation, including through sustainable consumption and production, sustainably managing its natural resources and taking urgent action on climate change, so that it can support the needs of the present and future generations.

Prosperity

We are determined to ensure that all human beings can enjoy prosperous and fulfilling lives and that economic, social and technological progress occurs in harmony with nature.

Peace

We are determined to foster peaceful, just and inclusive societies which are free from fear and violence. There can be no sustainable development without peace and no peace without sustainable development.

Partnership

We are determined to mobilize the means required to implement this Agenda through a revitalised Global Partnership for Sustainable Development, based on a spirit of strengthened global solidarity, focussed in particular on the needs of the poorest and most vulnerable and with the participation of all countries, all stakeholders and all people.

The interlinkages and integrated nature of the Sustainable Development Goals are of crucial importance in ensuring that the purpose of the new Agenda is realised.

If we realize our ambitions across the full extent of the Agenda, the lives of all will be profoundly improved and our world will be transformed for the better.

https://sustainabledevelopment.un.org/post2015/transformingourworld

Revelation 12

The Woman and the Dragon

12 A great sign appeared in heaven: a woman clothed with the sun,
with the moon under her feet and a crown of twelve stars on her
head. [2] She was pregnant and cried out in pain as she was about to
give birth. [3] Then another sign appeared in heaven: an enormous
red dragon with seven heads and ten horns and seven crowns on its

heads. [4] Its tail swept a third of the stars out of the sky and flung them
to the earth. The dragon stood in front of the woman who was about
to give birth, so that it might devour her child the moment he was
born.

[5] She gave birth to a son, a male child, who "will rule all the na-
tions with an iron scepter." And her child was snatched up to God
and to his throne. [6] The woman fled into the wilderness to a place
prepared for her by God, where she might be taken care of for 1,260
days.

[7] Then war broke out in heaven. Michael and his angels fought
against the dragon, and the dragon and his angels fought back. [8] But
he was not strong enough, and they lost their place in heaven. [9] The
great dragon was hurled down—that ancient serpent called the devil,
or Satan, who leads the whole world astray. He was hurled to the
earth, and his angels with him.

[10] Then I heard a loud voice in heaven say:

"Now have come the salvation and the power
and the kingdom of our God,
and the authority of his Messiah.
For the accuser of our brothers and sisters,
who accuses them before our God day and night,
has been hurled down.
[11] They triumphed over him
by the blood of the Lamb
and by the word of their testimony;
they did not love their lives so much
as to shrink from death.

12 Therefore rejoice, you heavens
and you who dwell in them!
But woe to the earth and the sea,
because the devil has gone down to you!
He is filled with fury,
because he knows that his time is short."

13 When the dragon saw that he had been hurled to the earth, he
pursued the woman who had given birth to the male child. 14 The
woman was given the two wings of a great eagle, so that she might
fly to the place prepared for her in the wilderness, where she would
be taken care of for a time, times and half a time, out of the serpent's
reach. 15 Then from his mouth the serpent spewed water like a river,
to overtake the woman and sweep her away with the torrent. 16 But
the earth helped the woman by opening its mouth and swallowing
the river that the dragon had spewed out of his mouth.

17 Then the dragon was enraged at the woman and went off to wage
war against the rest of her offspring—those who keep God's com-
mands and hold fast their testimony about Jesus.

Revelation 13

The Beast out of the Sea

13 The dragon stood on the shore of the sea. And I saw a beast com-
ing out of the sea. It had ten horns and seven heads, with ten crowns
on its horns, and on each head a blasphemous name. 2 The beast I saw

resembled a leopard, but had feet like those of a bear and a mouth
like that of a lion. The dragon gave the beast his power and his throne
and great authority. 3 One of the heads of the beast seemed to have
had a fatal wound, but the fatal wound had been healed. The whole
world was filled with wonder and followed the beast. 4 People wor-
shiped the dragon because he had given authority to the beast, and
they also worshiped the beast and asked, "Who is like the beast? Who
can wage war against it?"

5 The beast was given a mouth to utter proud words and blasphe-
mies and to exercise its authority for forty-two months. 6 It opened
its mouth to blaspheme God, and to slander his name and his dwell-
ing place and those who live in heaven. 7 It was given power to wage
war against God's holy people and to conquer them. And it was given
authority over every tribe, people, language and nation. 8 All inhabit-
ants of the earth will worship the beast—all whose names have not
been written in the Lamb's book of life, the Lamb who was slain from
the creation of the world.

9 Whoever has ears, let them hear.

10 "If anyone is to go into captivity,
into captivity they will go.
If anyone is to be killed with the sword,
with the sword they will be killed."

This calls for patient endurance and faithfulness on the part of God's people.

The Beast out of the Earth

11 Then I saw a second beast, coming out of the earth. It had two
horns like a lamb, but it spoke like a dragon. 12 It exercised all the

authority of the first beast on its behalf, and made the earth and
its inhabitants worship the first beast, whose fatal wound had been
healed. [13] And it performed great signs, even causing fire to come
down from heaven to the earth in full view of the people. [14] Because
of the signs it was given power to perform on behalf of the first beast,
it deceived the inhabitants of the earth.

It ordered them to set up an image in honour of the beast who was
wounded by the sword and yet lived. [15] The second beast was given
power to give breath to the image of the first beast, so that the image
could speak and cause all who refused to worship the image to be
killed.

[16] It also forced all people, great and small, rich and poor, free and
slave, to receive a mark on their right hands or on their foreheads, [17] so
that they could not buy or sell unless they had the mark, which is the
name of the beast or the number of its name.

[18] This calls for wisdom. Let the person who has insight calculate
the number of the beast, for it is the number of a man. That number
is 666.

Babylon the Great, Revelation 17,18,19: 1-9

Revelation 17

Babylon, the Prostitute on the Beast

17 One of the seven angels who had the seven bowls came and said

to me, “Come, I will show you the punishment of the great prosti-
tute, who sits by many waters. 2 With her the kings of the earth com-
mitted adultery, and the inhabitants of the earth were intoxicated
with the wine of her adulteries.”

3 Then the angel carried me away in the Spirit into a wilderness.
There I saw a woman sitting on a scarlet beast that was covered with
blasphemous names and had seven heads and ten horns. 4 The wom-
an was dressed in purple and scarlet, and was glittering with gold,
precious stones and pearls. She held a golden cup in her hand, filled
with abominable things and the filth of her adulteries. 5 The name
written on her forehead was a mystery:

BABYLON THE GREAT

THE MOTHER OF PROSTITUTES

AND OF THE ABOMINATIONS OF THE EARTH.

6 I saw that the woman was drunk with the blood of God’s holy
people, the blood of those who bore testimony to Jesus.

When I saw her, I was greatly astonished. 7 Then the angel said to
me: “Why are you astonished? I will explain to you the mystery of the
woman and of the beast she rides, which has the seven heads and ten
horns. 8 The beast, which you saw, once was, now is not, and yet will
come up out of the Abyss and go to its destruction. The inhabitants of
the earth whose names have not been written in the book of life from
the creation of the world will be astonished when they see the beast,
because it once was, now is not, and yet will come.

9 “This calls for a mind with wisdom. The seven heads are seven
hills on which the woman sits. 10 They are also seven kings. Five have
fallen, one is, the other has not yet come; but when he does come, he

must remain for only a little while. [11] The beast who once was, and
now is not, is an eighth king. He belongs to the seven and is going to
his destruction.

[12] "The ten horns you saw are ten kings who have not yet received
a kingdom, but who for one hour will receive authority as kings along
with the beast. [13] They have one purpose and will give their power
and authority to the beast. [14] They will wage war against the Lamb,
but the Lamb will triumph over them because he is Lord of lords and
King of kings—and with him will be his called, chosen and faithful
followers."

[15] Then the angel said to me, "The waters you saw, where the pros-
titute sits, are peoples, multitudes, nations and languages.[16] The beast
and the ten horns you saw will hate the prostitute. They will bring her
to ruin and leave her naked; they will eat her flesh and burn her with
fire. [17] For God has put it into their hearts to accomplish his purpose
by agreeing to hand over to the beast their royal authority, until God's
words are fulfilled.

[18] The woman you saw is the great city that rules over the kings of
the earth."

Revelation 18

Lament Over Fallen Babylon

18 After this I saw another angel coming down from heaven. He had
great authority, and the earth was illuminated by his splendor.[2] With

a mighty voice he shouted:
"'Fallen! Fallen is Babylon the Great!'
She has become a dwelling for demons
and a haunt for every impure spirit,
a haunt for every unclean bird,
a haunt for every unclean and detestable animal.
3 For all the nations have drunk
the maddening wine of her adulteries.
The kings of the earth committed adultery with her,
and the merchants of the earth grew rich from her excessive luxuries."

Warning to Escape Babylon's Judgment

4 Then I heard another voice from heaven say:
"'Come out of her, my people,
so that you will not share in her sins,
so that you will not receive any of her plagues;
5 for her sins are piled up to heaven,
and God has remembered her crimes.
6 Give back to her as she has given;
pay her back double for what she has done.
Pour her a double portion from her own cup.
7 Give her as much torment and grief
as the glory and luxury she gave herself.
In her heart she boasts,

‘I sit enthroned as queen.
I am not a widow;
I will never mourn.’
8 Therefore in one day her plagues will overtake her:
death, mourning and famine.
She will be consumed by fire,
for mighty is the Lord God who judges her.

Threefold Woe Over Babylon’s Fall

9 “When the kings of the earth who committed adultery with her and shared her luxury see the smoke of her burning, they will weep and mourn over her.
10 Terrified at her torment, they will stand far off and cry:

“‘Woe! Woe to you, great city,
you mighty city of Babylon!
In one hour your doom has come!’

11 “The merchants of the earth will weep and mourn over her because no one buys their cargoes anymore—
12 cargoes of gold, silver, precious stones and pearls; fine linen, purple, silk and scarlet cloth; every sort of citron wood, and articles of every kind made of ivory, costly wood, bronze, iron and marble;
13 cargoes of cinnamon and spice, of incense, myrrh and frankincense, of wine and olive oil, of fine flour and wheat; cattle and sheep; horses and carriages; and human beings sold as slaves.

14 “They will say, ‘The fruit you longed for is gone from you.

All your luxury and splendour have vanished, never to be recov-
ered.' [15] The merchants who sold these things and gained their wealth
from her will stand far off, terrified at her torment. They will weep
and mourn[16] and cry out:

"'Woe! Woe to you, great city,
dressed in fine linen, purple and scarlet,
and glittering with gold, precious stones and pearls!
[17] In one hour such great wealth has been brought to ruin!'

"Every sea captain, and all who travel by ship, the sailors, and all
who earn their living from the sea, will stand far off. [18] When they see
the smoke of her burning, they will exclaim, 'Was there ever a city
like this great city?' [19] They will throw dust on their heads, and with
weeping and mourning cry out:

"'Woe! Woe to you, great city,
where all who had ships on the sea
became rich through her wealth!
In one hour she has been brought to ruin!'
[20] "Rejoice over her, you heavens!
Rejoice, you people of God!
Rejoice, apostles and prophets!
For God has judged her
with the judgment she imposed on you."

The Finality of Babylon's Doom

[21] Then a mighty angel picked up a boulder the size of a large mill-

stone and threw it into the sea, and said:
"With such violence
the great city of Babylon will be thrown down,
never to be found again
22 The music of harpists and musicians, pipers and trumpeters,
will never be heard in you again.
No worker of any trade
will ever be found in you again.
The sound of a millstone
will never be heard in you again.
23 The light of a lamp
will never shine in you again.
The voice of bridegroom and bride
will never be heard in you again.
Your merchants were the world's important people.
By your magic spell all the nations were led astray.
24 In her was found the blood of prophets and of God's holy people,
of all who have been slaughtered on the earth."
Revelation 19:

Threefold Hallelujah Over Babylon's Fall

After this I heard what sounded like the roar of a great multitude in heaven shouting:

"Hallelujah!
Salvation and glory and power belong to our God,

2 for true and just are his judgments.
He has condemned the great prostitute
who corrupted the earth by her adulteries.
He has avenged on her the blood of his servants."
3 And again they shouted:
"Hallelujah!
The smoke from her goes up for ever and ever."
4 The twenty-four elders and the four living creatures fell down and worshiped God, who was seated on the throne. And they cried:
"Amen, Hallelujah!"
5 Then a voice came from the throne, saying:
"Praise our God,
all you his servants,
you who fear him,
both great and small!"
6 Then I heard what sounded like a great multitude, like the roar of rushing waters and like loud peals of thunder, shouting:
"Hallelujah!
For our Lord God Almighty reigns.
7 Let us rejoice and be glad
and give him glory!
For the wedding of the Lamb has come,
and his bride has made herself ready.
8 Fine linen, bright and clean,
was given her to wear."
(Fine linen stands for the righteous acts of God's holy people.)
9 Then the angel said to me, "Write this: Blessed are those who are

invited to the wedding supper of the Lamb!" And he added, "These are the true words of God."

10 At this I fell at his feet to worship him. But he said to me, "Don't do that! I am a fellow servant with you and with your brothers and sisters who hold to the testimony of Jesus. Worship God! For it is the Spirit of prophecy who bears testimony to Jesus."

The Heavenly Warrior Defeats the Beast

11 I saw heaven standing open and there before me was a white horse, whose rider is called Faithful and True. With justice he judges and wages war. 12 His eyes are like blazing fire, and on his head are many crowns. He has a name written on him that no one knows but he himself. 13 He is dressed in a robe dipped in blood, and his name is the Word of God. 14 The armies of heaven were following him, riding on white horses and dressed in fine linen, white and clean. 15 Coming out of his mouth is a sharp sword with which to strike down the nations. "He will rule them with an iron scepter."[a] He treads the winepress of the fury of the wrath of God Almighty. 16 On his robe and on his thigh he has this name written:

KING OF KINGS AND LORD OF LORDS.

17 And I saw an angel standing in the sun, who cried in a loud voice to all the birds flying in midair, "Come, gather together for the great supper of God, 18 so that you may eat the flesh of kings, generals, and the mighty, of horses and their riders, and the flesh of all people, free and slave, great and small."

19 Then I saw the beast and the kings of the earth and their armies gathered together to wage war against the rider on the horse and his army. 20 But the beast was captured, and with it the false prophet who had performed the signs on its behalf. With these signs he had deluded those who had received the mark of the beast and worshiped its image. The two of them were thrown alive into the fiery lake of burning sulfur. 21 The rest were killed with the sword coming out of the mouth of the rider on the horse, and all the birds gorged themselves on their flesh.

Revelation 20

The Thousand Years

And I saw an angel coming down out of heaven, having the key to the Abyss and holding in his hand a great chain. 2 He seized the dragon, that ancient serpent, who is the devil, or Satan, and bound him for a thousand years. 3 He threw him into the Abyss, and locked and sealed it over him, to keep him from deceiving the nations anymore until the thousand years were ended. After that, he must be set free for a short time.

4 I saw thrones on which were seated those who had been given authority to judge. And I saw the souls of those who had been beheaded because of their testimony about Jesus and because of the word of God. They had not worshiped the beast or its image and had not received its mark on their foreheads or their hands. They came to

life and reigned with Christ a thousand years. [5] (The rest of the dead did not come to life until the thousand years were ended.) This is the first resurrection. [6] Blessed and holy are those who share in the first resurrection. The second death has no power over them, but they will be priests of God and of Christ and will reign with him for a thousand years.

Printed in Great Britain
by Amazon

61696253R00109